You CAN Go to Church on Sunday
AND
Vote For Barack Obama on Tuesday

by

Dan Bimrose

For my beautiful wife Lindsay. It has been an amazing "fling." I could never begin to repay what I owe you. All my love.

also by Dan Bimrose

a novel

Max Yasgur's Farm

contact:

dan@bimrosemedia.com

website:

http://www.bimrosemedia.com

blogs:

http://www.liberalfix.com

http://www.proudliberalchristian.com

social media:

facebook.com/liberalfix

twitter.com - @danbimrose

Acknowledgements

Special thanks to Denver and Torrie for providing a couple more sets of eyes, always making me laugh and never letting me have an empty glass.

A project like this always takes time and I must always acknowledge those who are affected by such a committment. Much love and appreciation to my wife Lindsay and my five children Tyler, Dylan, Quinn, Libby and Johnna.

Topics such as this can bring up heated arguments and increased tensions within a family. I am thankful for my brothers and sisters and my wife's mother, brother and sisters for always remembering that family is the most important thing. Thanks for loving me regardless of what I may think. Besides, why talk politics when we can talk football instead?

To my many friends and colleagues I have come into contact with, I appreciate your commitment to your ideals and your relentless efforts to fight for the least amongst us. We should always endeavor to provide a voice for the voiceless.

As always, thanks Mom. You're the best.

"¹⁰ You, then, why do you judge your brother or sister? Or why do you treat them with contempt? For we will all stand before God's judgment seat. ¹¹ It is written:

"'As surely as I live,' says the Lord,

'every knee will bow before me; every tongue will acknowledge God.'"

¹² So then, each of us will give an account of ourselves to God.

¹³ Therefore let us stop passing judgment on one another. Instead, make up your mind not to put any stumbling block or obstacle in the way of a brother or sister."

Romans 14:10-13 NIV

"I don't want to see religious bigotry in any form. It would disturb me if there was a wedding between the religious fundamentalists and the political right. The hard right has no interest in religion except to manipulate it."

Rev. Billy Graham

"I will never, by any word or act, bow to the shrine of intolerance, or admit a right of inquiry into the religious opinions of others."

Thomas Jefferson

CONTENTS

Hell Freezes Over

Many terms can be used to describe the 2008 Presidential election.
It was long, spirited, divisive and sometimes just downright nasty.
Whatever adjective you prefer there is one particular adjective that
is entirely accurate and that word is historic. After the primary
and after the candidates picked their running mates we knew that
we were either going to have either the first black President or the
first woman Vice-President.

Ultimately and decisively it would be determined that Barack
Obama would be our nation's 44th President. The world rejoiced
and marveled at the progress the United States had made.

There was renewed interest in our electoral process and that
interest drove record numbers of people to the polls. It seemed
that everyone had an opinion and most wanted to share their
opinion with you.

For me, the election meant a major shift in my political leanings.
At some point in 2008 this Republican had morphed, not into a
Democrat initially, but rather an independent voter who had
realized that the Republican Party had failed to field an acceptable
candidate.

I liked Obama and his ideas and he would prove to be rather adept at explaining those ideas during his campaign.

Yes, I had become a flip-flopper.

This change in philosophies was an eye-opening experience. For the first time in my life I was at odds with the majority of my family politically. It was not just my brothers and sisters, but also the family of my wife. My family votes Republican because they are fiscal conservatives. My wife's family votes Republican largely because they are social conservatives.

Voting Democrat meant I was also at odds with one aspect of my life that had become very important to me, my church. Because of my Kafkaesque political transformation I had unwittingly been saddled with personal responsibility for the blood of all unborn babies. It was suggested that I should not call myself a Christian if I were to cast my vote for the Democratic ticket. For obvious reasons, this concept of vote for McCain and be a good Christian or vote for Obama and burn in Hell did not sit well with me. I have a fair complexion and I burn easily. There would not be enough aloe vera if my fate included an adjoining room with Hitler and apparently FDR.

The idea that it was one way or the other did not seem just or right. Unbeknownst to me, somewhere along the line God had endorsed John McCain. Well not so much John McCain, but his running mate Sarah Palin. Many pro-life Christians were very excited about the advanced age of McCain and pledged to pray for his early demise so that Sarah Palin could ascend to her rightful position as leader of the free world. These same pro-life Christians would very soon have no problem dreaming about the assassination of President Obama. Assassinate sounds far less sinister than using the word murder.

When I had voted Republican in the past I was coincidentally on the side of righteousness and therefore, I was unfazed by the attacks of the Christian right. It was only once I became one of "them" that I realized there was a politically important perceived difference in righteousness between the two parties.

This book details exactly the path that would lead this former Republican voter to cast my one vote for the enemy, aka Barack Hussein Obama.

I also will attempt to explain how I have the nerve to still call myself a Christian and I will reveal that, even to this day, I have never once burst into flames upon entering a church.

Even though my credentials currently include Bimrose Progressive Media (bimrosemedia.com) founder which manages our flagship website and blog liberalfix.com and Huffington Post contributor, you may be wondering how I could possibly be so conceited as to think that anyone would be even slightly interested in what I have to say about the influence of religion in politics.

If you will allow me I will reply with another question. Who would have thought anybody would have given a damn about what some fake plumber named Sam Wurzelbacher from the great state of Ohio had to say?

Unlike Joe the plumber, the mascot for the McCain/Palin team, I want you to rest assured that my motivation is not to further a career in music and I do not have a list of public relations firms printed up and ready to go in case I want to start contemplating a political career.

Although it is rather easy, it is not my aim to pick on Joe the plumber. He must be reasonably intelligent since he was able to explain the definition of "queer" to the rest of America. Unfortunately for him, I also looked up the word ignorant in the dictionary and the resemblance is uncanny.

As Joe the plumber and the 2008 election faded away we would discover that the fun had just begun.

When the voters elected a black man named Barack Obama to the Presidency, Hell had not frozen over, but you would have thought it had.

On Separation of Church and State

It has become a popular refrain among the religious right that all of our nation's problems exist because there is not enough Christianity in our government and in our schools. If we were only to mandate prayer in schools and arm our teachers with Bibles then certainly all that ails us would be healed. That if only our government were a bit more holy, all of our financial woes would disappear and the hurricanes would cease to blow and the earthquakes would cease to tremble.

The nation of China is currently kicking our proverbial economic behinds and has youth which rank number one in all relevant categories of education. Should we take those facts to mean that China, which is guilty of numerous human rights violations, is also holier than thou?

I am a proud unshakeable member of the Christian left, yet I find it amazing that many people refuse to accept this "crazy" notion that government has no role to play concerning religion except to assure that we all have the right to worship as we choose.

I have a hunch that the same people who believe that this so called recent diversion from God is directly attributable to the present administration in the White House are the same ones who believe that President Obama is deserving of the entirety of blame for the current economic environment.

The 2012 field of Republican presidential candidates included many disciples of the professor of revisionist history, David Barton. Candidates such as Rick Santorum, Michele Bachmann, and Rick Perry used their conservative Christian beliefs as a very effective tool to obtain votes and campaign donations.

All three have overtly stated their opposition to the separation of Church and State through either their words or their actions.

Using the same methods as David Barton to recreate history and rewrite the Constitution of the United States they have taken to the tactics of Fundamental Christians who must find a way to twist themselves into a pretzel trying to justify supporting someone who believes; a person should die if they don't have health insurance, that state sponsored executions are worthy of hearty applause, or that "real" American Republican Presidential candidates stay silent, sacrificing all decency, honor and integrity, when an audience boos an American soldier who is currently risking his life fighting for our country in Iraq for the sole reason that he is gay.

There are multiple sources of information which Christian conservatives can peruse to justify their fever for theocracy. These sources bend over backwards to push the belief that the Constitution only demands that Government stay out of the

Church and not the other way around.

They venture to the far reaches of their imagination to suggest that every one of our founding fathers intended that our government be subject to the Christian church. They simultaneously fail to acknowledge that when the founding fathers had the opportunity to make this desire obvious they chose not to do so.

Unfortunately for them the very first Amendment of the Constitution is nothing but clear that there should be a separation of Church and State. "Congress shall make no law respecting an establishment of religion, or prohibiting the free exercise thereof; or abridging the freedom of speech, or of the press; or the right of the people peaceably to assemble, and to petition the Government for a redress of grievances."

They shout that it does not say separation of Church and State. Who cares? The intent is obvious and the result is the same.

The Supreme Court has often used the words of our third President Thomas Jefferson, the author of the Declaration of Independence, to help them interpret and enable others to understand the intent of the very first Amendment. Contained in an 1802 letter to the Danbury Baptist Association from Jefferson were the following words, "Believing with you that religion is a matter which lies solely between Man & his God, that he owes account to none other for his faith or his worship, that the legitimate powers of government reach actions only, & not opinions, I contemplate with sovereign reverence that act of the whole American people which declared that their legislature should 'make no law respecting an establishment of religion, or prohibiting the free exercise thereof,' thus building a wall of separation between Church & State."

Less than ten years after the ratification of the Constitution, the treaty of Tripoli which was initiated by President George Washington, signed by President Adams and unanimously ratified by the Senate were the words, "As the Government of the United States of America is not, in any sense, founded on the Christian religion ..."

There is no recorded outrage expressed by the populace and no public debate over the painfully clear intent behind the inclusion of such words.

Why were there no protests held? Possibly for the simple reason that the fact that we are all free to worship as we choose is something to take pride in. Our forefathers had determined that we should all be free, not just some.

They understood that in order to keep the government out of religion that we must keep religion out of government. You cannot have one without the other.

James Madison is often referred to as the father of the Constitution and we find in the Annals of Congress the following statement from Madison: "Congress should not establish a religion and enforce the legal observation of it by law, nor compel men to worship God in any manner contrary to their conscience, or that one sect might obtain a pre-eminence, or two combined together, and establish a religion to which they would compel others to conform."

The thought occurred to me while contemplating the current state of public opinion, how weak and powerless some Christians must feel about our faith that they must task the Government with spreading the message that the rest of us have learned in our living rooms and in our churches. It was great comfort to me that another signer of the Constitution, Ben Franklin, expressed the same sentiment. "When religion is good, it will take care of itself. When it is not able to take care of itself, and God does not see fit to take care of it, so that it has to appeal to the civil power for support, it is evidence to my mind that its cause is a bad one."

While some Republican conservatives, such as Congressman Paul Ryan, express devotion to the currently very popular atheist Ayn Rand and her religion of selfishness, to a one they all also kneel at the altar of Ronald Reagan.

Many Republicans conveniently forget the fact that Reagan gave amnesty to illegal immigrants, raised taxes many times, orchestrated a substantial reduction in nuclear arms and left the nation in more debt than when he got there. They will also surely look past what President Reagan had to say about the separation of Church and State:

"We establish no religion in this country, we command no

worship, we mandate no belief, nor will we ever. Church and state are, and must remain, separate. All are free to believe or not believe, all are free to practice a faith or not, and those who believe are free, and should be free, to speak of and act on their belief. At the same time that our Constitution prohibits state establishment of religion, it protects the free exercise of all religions and walking this fine line requires government to be strictly neutral."

While some may prefer the idealized fiction of David Barton, I prefer the wisdom of Ben Franklin. While some stand behind Michele Bachmann, I shall stand with George Washington. While some look to Rick Perry for guidance, I look to Thomas Jefferson. While some prefer the intolerance of Rick Santorum, I shall enjoy the freedom to worship as I choose guaranteed to me by James Madison.

It is important for all to understand that my opinion in this matter makes me no less a Christian, nor no less an American. I fervently believe in my Christian home and my free nation.

Hoping and praying for a Christian theocracy means you are willing to forfeit our democracy which was only created and held together through the tremendous loss of life of many great and brave men. These men died so that all could be free and not that all shall be Christian.

By mandating that Christianity reign as the sole authority in Washington you will reduce the voice of others to a whisper and will have lost the right to sing the song about the "land of the free."

What is Fundamental Christianity and Why I Am Not a Fan

The roots of fundamentalism can be found in the early 20th century. Christian fundamentalism does not define a church but rather a belief that some elements are absolutely fundamental to being a true Christian. These elements are often doctrinal and have little to do with Christ's message.

Perhaps the most important belief is that the Bible represents truth in its entirety. There are no contradictions contained within and it is not subject to interpretation. Fundamentalists also believe that the Bible contains everything necessary to obtain salvation and holiness. They believe in the virgin birth, the resurrection, and for over 2000 years they have anticipated the imminent return of Christ. Each successive generation is assured that theirs is the generation in which Christ will return. They assert that he died so that we all may be forgiven.

Fundamentalism was a response to liberal theology. Many people may think that liberal is only a word used in politics to refer to people who think that we exist for the good of all, not for the good of ourselves only. Liberal can actually mean a variety of things, but suggests an inclination to think outside of the box and to not hold firm to a strict ideology and more importantly a tendency to not hold others to our same ideology. Open-mindedness is a virtue that should be cherished and not maligned.

In the case of theology, liberal refers to the idea that some may study the Bible and come to their own conclusions while not adhering to someone else's conclusions. A person who has liberal theological views generally has somewhat of a disdain for Christian dogma or Church doctrine. Dogma refers to an established belief that is not to be disputed and doctrine refers more specifically to an established belief by a certain church.

It is not uncommon to hear one say, "they are preaching against doctrine." When saying this it gives one the impression that their church's doctrine represents beliefs that are superior to the lessons we learn from Christ. If this were not true the person could simply say, "they are preaching against Christ."

It would be a mistake to assume that a fundamentalist and a liberal Christian are polar opposites. They do share some views in common. It would be accurate though, to say that one group tolerates opposing views and the other does not.

Perhaps more important, for the purposes of this book, than defining fundamentalist Christianity we should discuss how fundamentalist Christianity is perceived. Ultimately we must ask ourselves or perhaps they must ask themselves if the manner in which they approach Christianity could possibly inhibit the willingness of some to walk into a Church and receive Christ.

I have given a somewhat general outline of what fundamentalists believe, but let's look more at the specifics. How do their beliefs influence the debate on issues in the news today?

Fundamentalists believe that the earth was created in six twenty four hour periods. They believe in creation theory and emphatically oppose evolution. They believe the earth is only six to seven thousand years old.

They believe homosexuality is an abomination, a sickness, a choice, a sin and/or a sign that one's body or mind has come under the influence of Satan. They oppose increased penalties when courts consider a crime against a lesbian or gay individual.

They vehemently oppose legalization of abortion and consider making abortion illegal more important than actually lowering the abortion rate.

They oppose the use of birth control which is an obvious contradiction since the root cause of the vast majority of abortions performed today could very accurately be defined as the existence of an unplanned pregnancy.

They believe in a Christian nation state and they strongly believe in mandating prayer in schools as long as it is Christian prayer.

They believe that church leaders should be allowed to use the pulpit to push a political agenda.

They believe God routinely punishes us as a nation for abortion, homosexuality and all forms of sexual sin through the use of natural disasters.

They hold scientific evidence in low regard and consider much of it to be no more than hocus pocus.

We could go on and on naming their controversial opinions. I disagree with the majority of these opinions and beliefs. Because of this I am deemed to be just as guilty, just as bad, just as much a sinner, just as possessed as one of those evil "gays" or "baby killers".

The fact that I am not in agreement with them would lead them to determine that I am, at worst, a non-Christian and at best a bad Christian.

What is a Christian? People have a vast difference in opinion on this question, but most simply, a Christian is a follower of Christ. What do Christians hope to attain? The ultimate goal is everlasting life and a pass on judgment day. How do we get there? Jesus tells us himself in Luke.

> 25 On one occasion an expert in the law stood up to test Jesus. "Teacher," he asked, "what must I do to inherit eternal life?"
>
> 26 "What is written in the Law?" he replied. "How do you read it?"
>
> 27 He answered, "'Love the Lord your God with all your heart and with all your soul and with all your strength and with all your mind'; and, 'Love your neighbor as yourself.'"
>
> 28 "You have answered correctly," Jesus replied. "Do

this and you will live." (Luke 10:25-28 NIV)

Pretty simple really, take the above steps and you are "saved." Fundamentalists would argue that this is too simple.

It seems that many, not just fundamentalists, have ventured away from the teachings of Christ and instead are now focused on dogma and doctrine. In other words they emphasize what their individual church dictates to be true over the message that Christ preached.

While many wish to push the false narrative with obvious implications that we need to put Christ back in Christmas I am starting to believe that we need to put Christ and his message back into America's churches. In essence, we need to put Christ back into Christianity.

Instead of advocating for an all encompassing congregation of believers, fundamentalists seek only those who look, talk, and act as they do. They do not want their reputation tarnished by associating with sinners and non-believers. I cannot think of a more "un-Christ like" position than this. Anybody who holds this position demonstrates a complete inability to understand Christ's message.

Fundamentalists will argue that their positions are not controversial and are entirely mainstream America. They truly believe this. If you are knowledgeable and can demonstrate that their views are not mainstream America they will argue that they are right and everyone else is wrong. I might add that everyone else is headed for a fiery damnation in hell.

That their opinions are controversial is the root cause for why they receive so much attention from the media. They are loud, proud and most importantly good for ratings.

In August of 2011, Presidential hopeful Rick Perry, the state of Texas and a variety of controversial Christian organizations hosted an event they called the Day of Prayer. The event chose as speakers some pastors with questionable teachings.

The Day of Prayer was funded by the American Family Association which holds as one of their beliefs that America's right to religious freedom only applies to Christians.

Mike Bickle brought his group International House of Prayer to the event. Mike Bickle once said this about Oprah, "I believe that one of the main pastors, as a forerunner to the Harlot movement, it's not the Harlot movement yet, is Oprah. She is winsome, she is kind, she is reasonable, she is utterly deceived, utterly deceived. A classy woman, a cool woman, a charming woman, but has a spirit of deception and she is one of the clear pastors, forerunners to the Harlot movement."

The guy who John McCain once sought for his endorsement and then declined his endorsement, John Hagee also endorsed the Day of Prayer. He once preached that Adolf Hitler was sent by God to hunt Jews in order to send them to the Promised Land.

Hagee's exact words, "Then God sent a hunter. A hunter is

someone with a gun and he forces you. Hitler was a hunter. And the Bible says, Jeremiah writing, *'They shall hunt them from every mountain and from every hill and from the holes of the rocks,'* meaning there's no place to hide. And that might be offensive to some people but don't let your heart be offended. I didn't write it, Jeremiah wrote it. It was the truth and it is the truth. How did it happen? Because God allowed it to happen. Why did it happen? Because God said my top priority for the Jewish people is to get them to come back to the land of Israel."

The fact that these people are the headliners for the Christian faith creates real problems. If this is the only type of behavior that non-believers and those curious about Christianity see, it means that there are millions of people who will not walk into a church because they believe we are all like this, we all think like this, and we all talk like this.

Let me be clear, this is not the case. Even though the intent of this book is not to discredit fundamentalism, if I end up establishing the ability of those of us who do not follow all or any of the tenets of fundamentalism to be able to do so without feeling as if they are evil then that is a bonus.

If while fulfilling the purpose of this book I have allowed some to reconsider the effect that the words of Christ can have on their life then that is an additional bonus.

I must also acknowledge that some will readily respond to the fundamentalist message. Some will indeed be moved by their positions. These people are not the ones I am trying to reach. Fundamentalists will always get their followers.

It is everyone else that I am concerned about, but fully justifying and arguing on the behalf of liberal theology is for another book.

As Fundamentalism continues to creep into American politics and our conservative leaders continue to be beholden to the votes and money associated with Fundamentalism we must consider the possibility that some will endeavor to restrict our right to religious freedoms and seek to perpetuate their own views as the only view.

The fact that those who practice Liberal Christianity and those who practice Fundamental Christianity differ on many things should not be seen as a problem, but rather as a tremendous testament to the ultimate wisdom of our founding fathers who decided that it is not the responsibility of government to teach us how to worship, but to allow us to worship as we will.

Grandpa Gerry

I entered this world as a white, middle-class, conservative Republican. My family was extremely Catholic and thus at odds with the debatable Catholic tradition of leaning Democrat. This served to underline the fact that we do not always have to conform to the ideas of the groups which provide the foundations for our life.

Most children start out supporting the same party as their mother and father. My parents fed me and fed me well. Who was I to argue? I was not much of a rebel and I never really considered changing my loyalties just to piss them off.

The first President that I remember was Gerald Ford. I liked him for what I must have thought were good reasons at the time. My parents liked him and he looked like someone who would be a good grandpa.

I have a long tradition of staying up for the results on election night. I was seven years old the night that the peanut farmer Jimmy Carter beat the guy I would have loved to have for a grandfather. Initially I was devastated and then I went to play with my Six Million Dollar Man action figure.

Eventually multiplication tables and the girl who sat next to me in class every day would consume my every thought and I would learn that not much in life changes for a seven year old when the party in power in the White House changes hands.

As the years rolled on I became more knowledgeable about the way the world works. I can vividly remember having a discussion with my father about socialism when I was around the age of twelve years old. It seemed to me even then, that we already had an array of social programs and had for quite some time.

As much as I liked Gerry Ford I disdained Jimmy Carter. I was mystified as to why the lines at the pumps were so long at the gas station and why he could not bring home the Iranian hostages.

My political activism started while I was in fifth grade. Me and a friend of mine organized and staged a "Free the Hostages" day at school. As part of the festivities we sent a letter to the President pledging our support.

I was still somewhat limited in my knowledge of the way the world works, but I was getting the distinct impression that things were not good under the reign of the peanut farmer from Georgia.

Even though the Ayatollah was not impressed with my organizational abilities, he was impressed by one thing or rather one person, Ronald Reagan. After defeating Jimmy Carter and on his Inauguration day the hostages were released.

Ronald Reagan was first and foremost a motivator and a

communicator. He seemed to restore morale and faith in our country.

His communication skills were extraordinary. This was something that John McCain could have used when running for President in 2008. Reagan was able to explain how trickle-down economics or Reaganomics was supposed to work. He explained it to those of us in the middle class. If you deregulate you will create opportunity for growth in industry and if you give the corporations more money and relieve some of the tax burden you will further increase that growth. Allow the corporations to spend more money on expanding their business and that will create new job opportunities at home and increase our average income.

On the surface it seemed to make sense. Little did we know that this economic theory would result in stagnant growth, an even smaller middle class and shrinking wages.

Let us fast forward to the first President Bush. His one and only term was relatively non-eventful. His undoing was the phrase "no new taxes." He sealed his fate not when he uttered those words, but when he broke the promise.

The door of opportunity was open for an emerging young Democrat. For me the fact that Bill Clinton could play a sax was his only redeeming quality. I spent the next eight years badmouthing Bill Clinton at every opportunity.

Clinton's Presidency started with his decision to hand the reigns of health care reform over to his wife. It is true that Hillary Clinton was not an ordinary First Lady; she was highly intelligent and had a successful career of her own. Prior to Hillary, the President's significant other was typically saddled with no more responsibility than promoting a social cause and the design of the Presidential china.

At that time I felt that the responsibility for implementing a major policy change should not be handed off to the spouse of the President. Whether I was right or wrong, her efforts ultimately resulted in failure.

Eventually we would hear a great deal about cigars and a White House intern named Monica Lewinsky. The Lewinsky debacle was without a doubt an embarrassment to our country. It was an issue that we should not have had to deal with. Yes Bill Clinton is also just a man, but we should expect more from our President.

As a Republican I did have difficulty dealing with the fact that under the guidance of the Clinton administration the economy soared and jobs were created. The explanation most of us Republicans offered was that he did not screw up what Ronald Reagan had started. Perhaps he was just smart enough to follow the old adage, "if it ain't broke, don't fix it."

He did in fact balance the budget, albeit with the encouragement of a Republican Congress. Clinton could be labeled a fiscal conservative. The fact that a Democratic President was able to balance the budget was vital to me when it came time to consider voting for a Democratic candidate in 2008.

Following Clinton to the White House as we all know was George W. Bush. He seemed to me at that time to be a good choice for President and I was certainly happy to have anyone but Al Gore in the office even if the Supreme Court was the one who would ultimately decide the election.

Gore did not have Bill Clinton's charismatic gifts, but in retrospect he likely would have provided far less material for the late night talk show hosts than the eventual winner.

George W. Bush was not exactly quick on his feet or a master orator, but he was a Republican and that was all that mattered to me.

If W. had not performed well immediately following 9/11 his chances in 2004 would have been far more limited.

The list of his failures is monumentally long and I have no desire to delve into all of them. My biggest problem with his run as President was tossing aside the balanced budget that Bill Clinton had attained.

If we follow accepted stereotypes Democrats are not supposed to balance budgets, Republicans are. Republicans are not supposed to increase spending, Democrats are. In this case stereotypes had very little to do with reality.

The increased spending was due in large part to our wars with Iraq and Afghanistan. In regards to the Iraq war we now know that it was begun, if not with lies, then with incredibly false intelligence. Because of this, Iraq was a war of choice, a war where thousands of American lives were needlessly and senselessly lost. Iraq was a war that placed our nation's finances at great risk.

Let me be clear on one thing. At the onset of these wars I was in support of them. Over time after I saw what these wars were costing our country in the form of lives lost and loans from the Chinese, my mind changed. I became angry that we may have been misled or that the billions we spend annually on intelligence provided us with bogus information. Having said this, I am 110% in support of our troops that are fighting this war. They have my utmost respect and admiration.

Republicans will argue that there is no way to measure the amount of American lives that were saved by waging these wars "on terror". Quite frankly and quite simply I do not believe this. If we have done anything by waging these wars we have solidified the extremist Muslim belief that it is them against us. There is also no way to quantify the number of lives that will be lost in the future due to our presence in the Middle East.

I do believe that we should have secured our borders and tactically attacked Taliban and Al Qaeda strongholds via missile, drone and bomber attacks. To attack a nation with few ties to Al Qaeda or the Taliban was foolish.

We did rid the world of a ruthless dictator and we can be proud of that. We have sent a message to Muslim extremists that we mean business. If you attack us we will come after you. The way I see it, we sent this message a long time ago. Today our men and women are still fighting and still dying.

To this very day the cost of the war threatens the strength of our economy. In order to fund this war, George W. Bush and Congress decided to lie in bed with the completely godless nation of China. The money that we have borrowed from them provides them with power over us. While they send us crap in the form of their underpriced and sometimes defective imports, we can do little to stop them.

Finally the last straw for me with President Bush, and the straw that broke John McCain's back was the economic crisis. While McCain continuously touted the only way to attain economic recovery was to cut taxes even further I looked at Bush's tax cuts and the fact that we were in the throes of a scary economic down turn and wondered if tax cuts were so crucial why did Bush's tax cuts not launch us into economic over-drive. After all, he cut taxes for the wealthiest Americans.

Momma always said, "don't throw good money after bad." Giving business and the wealthiest Americans an even greater tax break would do little or nothing. I understood what John McCain was talking about. It is the same policy that Ronald Reagan advocated for, but I do not think that most people appreciate that our nation and our economy is in a constant state of flux. What works during one period of time may not work for another.

Offering tax breaks is a passive solution. By giving business extra money in the hope that they will use it to expand their business and hire employees represents little more than a pipe dream. The benefit is not immediate and the results would not be seen for some time.

We did not have time to wait. We did not have time for John McCain and his policies. I had to consider voting for Barack Obama.

After thoroughly researching Senator Obama's plans I came to the conclusion that he represented our best chance. He had ideas and he had proactive solutions. He explained to us why they were needed and why they would work. He offered a concrete definable way out and not just a repeat of past mistakes.

I truly never thought that I would vote for a Democrat. The path that I traveled to that decision was truly a winding road. The experience that life offered and which is only attained by celebrating considerably more than twenty birthdays, taught me that my youthful ideals do not always represent the ideal solution.

These were things that I could not have learned without the benefit of having children, having a wife and trying to keep my head above water from year to year.

I believe with all my heart that inherent in our right for "life, liberty and the pursuit of happiness," is the ability to have adequate health coverage. Not having health coverage should not be an option for anyone. Whatever the cost, whatever it takes, all of us should have health coverage. The eight year old daughter of the poorest man should have the same coverage as the eight year old daughter of the richest man. No one should have to choose between receiving a life saving treatment and bankrupting their families.

I will never apologize for this belief and my resolve will never waver until our nation offers universal coverage.

During the last few years I have learned that a completely free market system without the restraints of regulation keeps the government out of business, but in its place greed comes to power. Greed becomes the master and the reigns are held by only a few people who wish to further their own interests at the expense of others. These few people will use everything at their disposal to push their agenda, including masking their agenda as entirely Christian inspired.

I will close with a fitting quote from the movie *Wall Street*. This is from Michael Douglas and his marvelous performance as Gordon Gecko:

> "The richest one percent of this country owns half our country's wealth, five trillion dollars. One third of that comes from hard work, two thirds comes from inheritance, interest on interest accumulating to widows and idiot sons and what I do, stock and real estate speculation. It's bullshit. You got ninety percent of the American public out there with little or no net worth. I create nothing. I own. We make the rules pal, the news, war, peace, famine, upheaval, the price per paper clip. We pick that rabbit out of the hat

while everybody sits out there wondering how the hell we did it. Now you're not naive enough to think we're living in a democracy, are you buddy?

Forgive Me Father Tom

The influences on my spirituality in my formative years were Catholic, Catholic, and Catholic. I have many fond memories of our Parish Priest, Father Tom and my experience in the Catholic Church.

Later, during college I took two religion classes, religions of the east and religions of the west. I did not expect these classes to shake my faith, nor did they.

After college I regularly attended a Pentecostal church pastored by a man whom I had the utmost respect for. I have never known anyone so dedicated to his faith and so persistent in his desire to follow those mandates he found in the Bible and those which were revealed to him in his daily meditations and study.

Shortly thereafter and not resulting from any negative religious experience, I came to believe that there was no God. I believed that there was no heaven and no hell. This is a rather egregious sin that, if I take the New Testament literally, offers me no hope for redemption. It was only due to the patient and persistent efforts of my wife Lindsay that I returned to a faith in God and found truth through the New Testament, particularly the Gospels, and the teachings of Jesus.

Obviously my spiritual path has not been a straight line. I do not think it is for most people, but I have certainly taken a considerably winding road.

It has been told to me by my mother that after my Christening guests remarked that there were probably more people in attendance at my very first Sacrament than there would be at my wedding. Depending on which wedding they were talking about they were right.

From the time I was born until I was approximately fourteen I think I missed attending Sunday Mass less than a handful of times. On vacation, one of the first things my parents would do was locate the local Catholic Church wherever we were visiting so that we could be in attendance on Sunday.

The importance of attending Mass in my family can best be demonstrated by an experience that occurred during the Blizzard of 1978 in my hometown of Lebanon, Indiana. Over thirty years later people still talk about that particular blizzard. I was nine years old and the best thing about that blizzard that I can remember is that school was canceled for two weeks. It was so extreme that the only things moving on the roads were tanks from the local armory.

The blizzard involved more than one snow storm, but there were windows of time when the snow stopped flying. On one particular

Sunday during a brief reprieve from the onslaught of snow my father called our local priest Father Tom. The purpose of the call was to find out if there would be Mass that morning. We learned that the priest has to offer mass even if there are no parishioners in attendance.

That was all my parents needed. My mother, father, and I bundled up and made the three to four mile journey to St. Joseph's Catholic Church on foot. Upon our arrival it was obvious that the only people who would be attending the service would be the three of us and because of this Father Tom invited us to sit on the altar with him while he performed the service. The memory of that day has not faded and I look on it with much fondness.

I went on to become what I felt at that time must have been a record for the oldest altar boy. I would eventually be confirmed and I thought that I would always be a good Catholic.

After all, we were the only church in town that had beer on tap in the church hall and none of the other church's had pastors that offered an annual trip to the Kentucky Derby. A trip that was not just about seeing the horses run, but more importantly to see if the size of your wallet grew if you bet the right horses. Do I really need to say anything about the bingo? With my limited teenage mentality Catholics knew how to have a good time and I could not imagine attending a church where they served grape juice instead of wine.

Yes, they were a little strict about marriage or rather divorce, but

I was only going to be married one time so that was a non-issue.

I have very little bad to say about my personal experience with the Catholic Church which will probably upset most "good" Christians. Many of whom do not even consider Catholics to be Christians even though there would never have been a Bible and the message of Jesus would more than likely never have reached them were it not for the efforts of the Catholic Church. That fact alone is deserving of some respect.

Ignorance of the history of the church, the origin of the Bible, and bad information is what fuels most people's arrogance when claiming that Catholics are not Christian.

Everyone that is Christian, but not Catholic are by definition Protestants, which means they must be protesting something and that something necessarily had to come prior to the existence of their own selective brand of Christianity.

I do have one memorably bad episode which would shape my thoughts on the Church until this day. Every so often we would have a visiting missionary priest come for a visit and talk about his work. One of these gentlemen was pure fire and brimstone. He talked about little else than our sins and ultimate destiny in hell. I wish I had walked out of church that day. I do not know why I did not, except I did not want to embarrass my family. I was also young and really had not developed enough self-confidence to take a stand.

One of my core beliefs is that if you have to use fear and guilt to make me do something or not do something and are not able to appeal to my intellect then there must be something wrong with your argument. This belief will eventually play a strong role for me in the election of 2008.

Much later it would not take long for me to realize that once I began attending a Pentecostal Church, that I was in for a bit of a culture shock. Yes, there was speaking in tongues and yes, there was "laying on" of hands. As I was soon to discover the New Testament allows for that. If it is in there, who was I to think it was silly or crazy?

As much respect as I had for the Catholic Church I had become married outside of the church. I had made the transition. I would never again regularly attend a Catholic church.

The most important lesson I would learn is that many people who call themselves Christians believe different things. Trying to figure out who was right seemed to be a daunting and seemingly overwhelming task.

Eventually I would sour on organized religion. Not just religion, but God as well. I became a non-believer. At the time it worked out well for me.

I had never embraced religion wholeheartedly because I feel hypocrites are some of our lowest life forms. I could never be as perfect as I felt that I had to be. I could not parade myself around as a righteous person when I knew that there were things that I did and ways I behaved that would suggest I was anything but righteous.

Becoming a non-believer made it easy to justify all the bad things that had happened to me. I no longer had to ask, "Why God?" Those things happened to me because there was no God. No one was looking out for me. I had to look out for myself and my own best interests.

I believed that there was no heaven and hell. You just died and that was all. All the people that were preaching on the TV were wasting their lives. There were countless millions of people who had placed their hope in a fantasy. Oh well, whatever it takes to give your life meaning and provide hope.

When I stood up and said, "No I do not believe in God," I no longer felt guilt for my sins. It did not matter anymore. I could live the most disgusting life and behave in the most despicable fashion and in the end I would be no worse off than if I had spent my life devoted to following the Ten Commandments. Do not get me wrong, I still felt a moral obligation to do good and be good, I just knew that my moments of weakness would not be accounted for later.

Basically I had reached a point where I realized that I was Christian because that was how my parents raised me. That was not a good enough reason. I needed more. Although I understood that when you follow any religion or even lack of religion that there is a certain level of faith that must exist. There would never be definitive proof.

Still though, I felt that we were not just an accident. Time spent outdoors and in nature are some of my most spiritual moments. It was hard for me to believe, when I sat on the beach and looked over the miles of water, and heard the roar of the waves as they pounded the shore, and witnessed the beauty of the sky when the sun is setting that it was all just an accident. If it was, then it was one hell of an accident.

Although, I did not believe in heaven and hell I knew that there was good and evil. I had witnessed both in my life. I could not help but think that there were "forces" that ruled over both. When behaving badly, whether it was drugs or something else I felt like I was being pulled in that direction. As if something wanted me to behave that way. What or who that was, I did not know, but I had a hunch that they or it were not acting in my own best interests.

It was not until I met my current wife that I began my walk back to God and to Jesus Christ.

It was not by her bashing me over the head or constantly preaching, witnessing, or nagging, but rather her quietly persistent nature that helped the process along. I think she knew that telling me I had to believe in God was not going to be effective and it would result in a disingenuous faith.

I began in earnest, an effort to find the answers that I needed. I knew what direction I was heading, but when I got there it was going to be on my terms and with my own set of beliefs not those of any particular pastor.

The Bible is not black and white. Many people have read and studied the Bible for decades and come to separate conclusions. To think that one person figured it all out and was definitively right in every instance is preposterous. When it comes to religion no one can be proven right or wrong.

There are two things that led me to believe once again in God. The first is the beauty and the wonder that exists in the nature which I just discussed and the second is the amazing set of circumstances that enable us to even exist. That human beings are able to learn at the level we do separates us from every other animal on the planet. We are truly incredible creations and I personally find it difficult to fathom that we are the product of an amazing set of coincidences. What would be the odds?

My faith in Jesus Christ resulted from recognizing the remarkable truth in his words. An absolute truth, that truth for me is that love reigns supreme. This is indeed a very hippie-like perspective, but one which I readily embrace and one that makes sense to me on a spiritual level.

As we are all children of God, Jesus was the son of God. I am a follower of Jesus Christ, not Paul or any of the other writers of the books in the New Testament. Jesus taught peace, love and tolerance. He sat with sinners and embraced them. He did not expect people to be perfect before they came to him. It may be a bit cliché, but it was through him that I was saved. The truth of Jesus and his message saved me in many ways. I am a Christian.

Since God endowed us with the capacity to learn and think for ourselves I felt compelled to put those skills to work by more thoroughly and thoughtfully reading the Bible. Let me be clear, I read the Bible. I did not rely on snippets from a daily calendar and I did not rely on selective scriptures from the power point screen at Church on Sunday. I studied the Bible. I do not think many "good" Christians offer the same respect to the "good book."

In the Catholic Church, I grew up with little emphasis placed on studying scripture.

Many protestant churches encourage reading the Bible, but ask that you leave interpretation of what it says to the pastor. What would be the point of that?

While some things are confusing, I think that I am perfectly capable of thinking for myself. I understand that any scripture can be looked at in multiple ways and can be argued differently while addressing the same piece of scripture. Relying on someone telling me what a scripture "really" means, suggests that I do not have the intelligence required to discern that meaning for myself.

There are a few problems that I have had with the teachings of the modern church. Teachings that I thought could not be right. It was only upon reading the Bible that I discovered there was something to the gut feelings I had always had. What churches taught as matters of doctrine could not be found in the Bible or were a function of laws set up in the Old Testament.

Many teachings are the result of some serious reading between the lines. These teachings have evolved and become engrained in minds over decades and have resulted in today's church members believing that the teaching comes from God, but in fact come from the church leaders and long existing traditional thought.

Most church's preach about the sin of pre-marital sex, yet do not stress it or disavow it because in today's society it has not proven to have been realistic for the lives of people in the pews. The people in the pews are important because they pay the electric bill, as well as the pastor's salary. How many people have been taught that pre-marital sex is wrong, but do it anyway? How many people know that you should not drink to excess or consume illegal drugs, but do it anyway? How easy it is to become a hypocrite.

Many church's feel it is their prerogative to judge and condemn certain people to a destination in a fiery hell. Yet salvation has nothing to do with what we do. Salvation is promised when you accept Jesus Christ as your savior and ask for forgiveness of your sins. That is it, nothing else. Being a good Christian does not make you more "savable." It just makes you a good Christian.

Some church leaders love to proclaim that every natural disaster is the result of God's punishment for our sins. Yet in the New Testament it is revealed, many times, that Jesus Christ was sent because the old ways of the Old Testament were not effective. The same God that destroyed Sodom and Gomorrah because of their sins provided a man, both perfectly divine and human so that we may know the way and truth and finally realize forgiveness for our past mistakes and sins. Receiving forgiveness is only the first step on a wonderful journey which brings you closer to the spirit and God every day. This was a new way. It was no longer mandated that we follow the laws of the Old Testament; instead we are now given a choice to accept Jesus Christ into our lives. It is stressed many, many, many times in the New Testament that following the old laws will not get you into Heaven.

I know my own limitations. Quite frankly they are many. I have come to the conclusion that I walk on dirt, not in the clouds, and certainly not on water. Right now, in this moment, I live in the world and not in heaven. I am tempted daily. I succumb every now and then.

Living in the world is a condition that only death releases us from. Complete surrender to God is difficult and unlikely, unless you are a monk. Being a slave to money is not good, but neither is irresponsibility when you have people to take care of. We have to exist in this world for now. We are taught by some that if you want something, you have to get it yourself. It is that "self" that causes the majority of our problems. We are taught by others that if you want something you simply ask God. My personal feeling is that it probably takes a little of both.

I believe strongly in the separation of Church and State. I think both of our political parties should strive to maintain this separation. I believe God cares much more about the health of his church than he does about the government of the United States.

In my opinion I believe Jesus Christ would be incensed that so many of the ultra-conservative church leaders are twisting his words to support judgment and condemnation thereby excluding those whom they judge from knowing God's grace.

I think Jesus Christ would be terribly confused as to how continuously attacking any group somehow will endear them to your ideas or make them believe that you love them.

Hatred masked as righteousness is still hatred.

Many out there, perhaps most, will say that I am wrong. They will proclaim that you must stand and shout. You must stand and point your finger and you must judge everyone who is not like you. I will surely find out one day, but as long as I am living I will err on the side of compassion and tolerance.

#

This concludes my journey along the winding path that I took to come to my current political and spiritual philosophies. I thought it important to demonstrate that while some people as they grow older may grow bitter and judgmental, others can grow more compassionate and tolerant.

I have certainly chosen a path of love and nothing in the Bible suggest that I will suffer in this life or the next because of this path.

February 10, 2007

At the age of forty five, a black man named Barack Hussein Obama had the audacity to declare his candidacy for the highest office in the United States.

The first term senator stood in front of the Old State Capitol in Illinois, and dared to invoke the words of Abraham Lincoln.

He had the nerve to go up against the Clinton political machine when most people thought that Hillary Clinton would be impossible to beat.

Who did this joker think he was? Did he think that America had forgotten about 9/11? Did he not think his middle name would be a problem? Heck, his first and last names would be enough to raise eyebrows.

I must admit on that day that I knew very little about Barack Obama. I felt this story was a minor one and that Obama would make only a minimal impact on the race for the future Democratic nominee.

Besides I was a Republican, I was far more concerned with who would be the Republican nominee.

At the conclusion of January 3, 2008 I began to pay attention. Barack Obama won the Iowa caucus. What in the world was going on?

I began to ask questions. Had the United States advanced to the point where we could elect a black President? After obtaining the "secret Muslim" descriptor, how could he overcome the anti-Muslim sentiment that many American's possessed? Did people not realize that he had no executive experience and his sole experience in national politics had been as a first term Senator?

My research began in earnest. As a Republican, it was important that I be able to argue intelligently with my Democrat friends.

I knew about Huckabee's fair tax and I thought I liked it. I knew about Romney's "expertise" on economic issues and I thought I liked that as well. I knew about McCain's history as a Senator and I had no use for him.

This Barack Obama person though, I still knew relatively little about. It was new material and I enthusiastically began my research.

Little did I know that what I would discover would be the beginnings of a change in my political loyalties. The knowledge I would learn would be necessary to refute false allegations about him. I would eventually be forced to defend this man from unfair attacks from people who possessed limited information from questionable sources.

As a good Republican I wanted to point out his legitimate policy faults, not disparage his character with lies.

A New American Disease

There is a new disease running rampant throughout the United States and seems to affect mainly people above the voting age of eighteen. No it is not the Swine Flu and it is certainly not lethal.

People particularly at risk are those who get their news primarily through personally selected and biased websites or one of those "fair and balanced" cable news channels. These same people also place an extraordinary amount of faith in the validity of forwarded texts and emails.

Someone with this disease will make statements with no basis in fact. They respond to fear tactics and suffer delusions that only people with this disease are "real Americans" and "good Christians."

The most notable symptoms are laziness and apathy. It is not that they lack interest in all things, but rather just one, the truth.

The beauty of cable television is that we are provided with many options. If we like fishing we can watch The Outdoor Channel. If we like Golf we can watch the Golf Channel.

The downside of cable television can also be the very same thing.

If we are Republican we tend to watch Fox News and if we are Democrat we tend to watch MSNBC. When we only get one side of the story we are not getting all the information.

The same thing goes with online news sources. If we are Republican we visit the conservative blog sites and if we are Democrats we find out what the liberals are blogging about. Once again we see just one side of the argument.

As humans we tend to only listen to what we want to hear. After all if you love rock music you are not going to turn on the local country station.

That type of selective listening is fine with music, but perhaps as an electorate we should be open to hearing both sides of the argument. An educated electorate is far more valuable than a blindly partisan electorate.

In the beginning I did not want to come to the defense of a Democrat such as Barack Obama. However, with the wild and incredulous accusations being spread around I felt compelled to defend him.

I do watch MSNBC news. I also try to balance it with spending a fair amount of time watching CNN which attempts to be non-partisan in their delivery of the news. In addition, since the passing of President Ford, I have secretly wished David Gergen could be my grandfather.

Anyone with a brain, whether they be conservative or liberal, if being honest with themselves, knows that the Fox News' moniker

"Fair and Balanced" is not an accurate description of the way they present news. We also know that MSNBC has more than a liberal bias.

As I am writing this I am struggling with my desire to present both news channels in the same light, but it is impossible. Judging from the title of this book it will be no surprise that I think that MSNBC does a far better job delivering the facts than Fox News. Those facts are often supported with video evidence or by citing sources. Of course this goes on at Fox News, but I feel to a lesser degree and only when the facts or rather how they interpret the facts, support their viewpoint.

Let me provide an example, if half of the country is in a winter emergency for a week they will crack sarcastic jokes about global warming, but during a warm winter season like many of us experienced in the 2011/2012 winter they will stay mum on global warming. Meanwhile there is no mention on MSNBC or CNN that a select period of weather conditions in a select area does anything to validate or invalidate the existence of global warming. Only one of these news channels could we suggest is trying to push an agenda based on a false premise.

Fox News offers up Greta Van Susteren, Sean Hannity, and Bill O'Reilly. MSNBC counters with Ed Schultz, Lawrence O'Donnell, and Rachel Maddow.

These shows are not *Meet the Press* and for the most part they do not claim to be, but the first time I heard Sean Hannity refer to himself as a journalist I burst out in uncontrollable laughter and then became determined to come up with a new term for what it is that he does and for who he is. Celebrulism and celebrulist is what I came up with.

On some level all six commentators can be referred to in this manner. These are celebrities. Their ratings are not based upon their unbiased presentation of the news, but rather on their personal bias, their personality, and how well they can entertain. Some sensationalize stories simply for the sake of being sensational. I am thinking of the ousted Glenn Beck on this last point.

Ultimately the true danger is not only watching entirely Fox News or MSNBC, but rather the blind faith that many put in their favorite celebrulists. Believing everything that comes out of their mouth is unwise, lazy and devastating to one's intellect. If someone says something that just does not sound right then you should check it out.

I will admit that I once upgraded my satellite package just so I could watch Fox News. I quite enjoyed at that time the environment portrayed on Fox & Friends. They are on the air when everyone else is asleep in my house. I felt almost as if we were hanging out together.

That all changed as the rhetoric for the 2008 election began heating up and it became painfully obvious that these early AM celebrulists on Fox News were participating in the rhetoric. They were passing off Republican talking points as news. I simply could not believe the things that were coming out of their mouths. The show I used to enjoy was now making me quite nauseous.

I lost respect for them. I no longer could trust them. I had to move on. I had to find some other source for my news because Fox was providing fewer and fewer credible instances of journalism.

I started wondering how these people could look at themselves in the mirror, but then I reasoned that it was probably far easier if they had previously looked at the money in their checking account.

The resulting distaste I had from Fox News becoming Conservative News was just one more step that would lead me to voting for a Democrat for the first time in the 2008 election. Not only did I vote for a Democrat, but I was quite proud to do so.

I was now even more compelled to find out about this Obama character.

Red Flags

Viral e-mails are great for on-line marketers, but can be poison to the concept of truth. It was true that I wanted to talk about policies, but I first had to dispense with some of the most outrageous claims presented in viral e-mails.

With the middle name of Hussein it was far too easy for the political right to make a connection between Islam and Obama. The connection was made in spite of the fact that, if you remember the issues of the campaign, we heard a great deal about Obama's membership in Trinity United Church of Christ and his relationship with the Reverend Jeremiah Wright.

Either he was under the influence of a racist pastor or he was a secret Muslim. Which was it? How can you be both?

The first incredulous story that I remember hearing was that Obama was sworn in on the Koran. It was not conceivable to me that in the pre-election environment that anyone who practiced Islam would even consider running for President. This to me was a red flag. This made me research this fact even further. Others simply repeated the same thing that was told to me as truth, without verifying the veracity of the statement.

He was actually sworn in on his family Bible. Bush's right hand man, Vice-President Dick Cheney administered the oath of office and I think he would have mentioned that little bit of information.

Another confusing accusation was that Barack Obama was not patriotic. I mean after all he was running for President of the United States. What was the basis for making this claim? He did not wake up in the morning with a flag pin on his lapel and he refused to put his hand over his heart when he said the Pledge of Allegiance.

To the first point I would like to ask a question. Who cares? When the heck did this tradition start and when did it become a required part of the uniform of a Presidential candidate? I have never worn a flag pin a day in my life and yet I consider myself a Patriot. You could say, yeah, but I expect more from my Presidential candidates. So why did you not expect more from Senator McCain because he did not wear one on a daily basis and appeared at two debates without a flag pin. No Presidential candidate regularly wore one except for Rudy Giuliani.

The second point concerning his refusal to put his hand over his heart during the Pledge of Allegiance is completely without basis in fact. Five minutes of research would reveal the one picture that I would eventually see dozens of times being cited as proof, was trumped by the dozens of pictures of Obama with his hand over the heart.

Interestingly enough the picture that haters use as evidence was actually taken during the singing of the Star Spangled Banner as an ABC video would prove. Shortly after the controversy several military leaders came out in support of Obama and defended him from these baseless attacks.

So he is not a Muslim and he is not unpatriotic, but is he the Anti-Christ. I will include one pathetic viral e-mail that I personally received as a text.

> "According to The Book of Revelations the anti-christ is: The anti-christ will be a man, in his 40s, of MUSLIM descent, who will deceive the nations with persuasive language, and have a MASSIVE Christ-like appeal....the prophecy says that people will flock to him and he will promise false hope and world peace, and when he is in power, will destroy everything is it OBAMA??"

The first problem with this is that the Book of Revelation never mentions the word "anti-Christ". How could this be, it is the book that describes the end times? Get out your Bible and check it out. I will always recommend that someone read their Bible to verify what others say. The word anti-Christ is never used, not once.

The next part of the e-mail that is utterly and completely false is that the Book of Revelation mentioned an age in reference to an anti-Christ. No age range was mentioned for an anti-Christ figure or anyone else for that matter. Once again scour the book for this and you will come up with nothing.

The most laughable assertion of this e-mail is that the Book of Revelation revealed that the anti-Christ is Muslim. Of course you cannot find this in the Book of Revelation since Islam was not even founded until more than 600 years after the birth of Jesus. It would be impossible for the Book of Revelation to mention Islam or describe someone as Muslim.

How can you trust people who disseminate these falsehoods? What would lead you to believe that they would ever have anything to offer that remotely resembles the truth? They have already indicated that they are either a willing liar or utterly ignorant.

Of course we cannot talk about viral e-mails without addressing the old tired "he's not a citizen" controversy.

On June 13, 2008 Barack Obama released his birth certificate. The Hawaii Department of Health stated that it was a valid birth certificate. Of course this was not good enough for many people. The conspiracy theorists went crazy.

Many did not think that Hawaii was really a state at the time of his birth. Thirty seconds on Google would have resolved this issue.

Many worried that the embossed seal and the registrar's signature appeared to be missing. They would have been on the back of the document.

Many were unhappy that it was not his original birth certificate.

I can tell you without a doubt that if someone would put a gun to my head and demand my original birth certificate that I would end up dead. Many people, if not most people would have a difficult time providing their original birth certificate.

The facts were that the document Barack Obama provided is valid for anything that you could possibly need a birth certificate, such as gaining a passport or providing proof of citizenship for a job even if that job is President of the United States.

Of course the President would eventually release the now infamous long form birth certificate after the controversy returned seemingly due in large part because of that great patriot and reality show host Donald Trump. Still conspiracy theorists would not be satisfied, but at least several politicians would now call off the witch hunt.

Possibly the most offensive emails were the racist emails. Many were jokes that were designed to be funny, but were utterly repulsive and revealed their senders to be bigots.

I really do not have much to say about these e-mails other than to state that if you base your opinion on any person solely on their skin then you are in fact a bigot and a racist and you should accept that fact.

You have revealed yourself to be ignorant, classless, without compassion, and better suited to live in the south during the 50's and 60's than anywhere in America in the 21st century.

An entire book could be devoted to the myths perpetuated

through the internet about Barack Obama. These e-mails were designed to make an impression on people who were ready and willing to be scared and easily deceived.

Since he was black and his middle name was Hussein there just had to be something wrong with him. He did not look like us and was not raised like us so there must be something wrong with him. He was different, therefore he was dangerous.

Some people are consumed with all manner of conspiracy theories. We cannot change these people. We can feel sorry for them, but we cannot change them.

While Defending Him, I Began To Like Him

Nearly every day it seemed there was some new allegation against the man who would eventually be President. I could not find evidence of any substance to support the petty accusations being tossed about by those wishing to stoke fear amongst the fearful.

While doing this research I was bound to learn more about what he advocated for and I found plenty. When I started listening to his speeches and studying his stances on policy I began to like him. Dare I say it, I began to respect him.

Senator Obama was speaking to me. John McCain was not. Barack Obama was speaking about providing security for the middle class. John McCain was not. John McCain was all about the war in Iraq. Barack Obama had voted against it. Obama stressed the importance of health care reform which would certainly help me and my family. McCain threw out some ideas about health care, but none of his ideas represented real effective change.

This last issue was something that was near and dear to my heart. I had worked for years for a company and utilized their employer provided health care. Year after year my healthcare costs continued to skyrocket.

It was almost like a bad joke. Every year at our all-employee meeting when it was time to talk about our health care they would ask the same thing, "Do you want the good news or the bad news?"

There would be a series of audible groans and then they would tell us, "Well, your premiums are going to stay the same but we are going to have to decrease your benefits." They would cut the benefits in the form of higher deductibles, co-pays and lowered annual and lifetime benefits.

One year they even told us that they would no longer be paying any claims from Children's Hospital in Cincinnati. If you were living in our area and your child had something seriously wrong then you were sent to Children's. Children's was the best. You would know your child was in good hands. This would no longer be an option and even though it did not affect me personally at the time I felt like it was a tragedy for many of my coworkers. How could they do this, I wondered?

The next year they would once again ask the question, "Do you want the good news or the bad news?" This time they would say we are going to leave your benefits alone but we are going to have to raise your premiums.

On alternating years they would continue to do one or the other. They would defend their actions by stating that our health insurance was still better and cheaper than what was offered to most Americans. They would present us with graphs showing the rising costs associated with health care. All I could think was that if we were better off than most, then the rest of the country was left with, for the lack of a better word, pure crap for health care. It was also becoming painfully obvious why the overwhelming majority of people who declared bankruptcy and cited health care debt as the reason had in fact been covered by employer provided health care insurance. Something was obviously very broken about our current system.

It was apparent that despite my one to two percent pay increase every year I was worse off than the year before just due to my increased health care costs. Factor in inflation on other items and I was certainly heading downhill financially every year. Was this the American dream or the American nightmare that I was living? It was no wonder that families needed two or three incomes just to maintain their standard of living.

The most important point that Barack Obama helped me to understand was that this was happening all over America to millions of families and this was having a devastating effect on our economy.

If everyone was losing personal disposable income then we were increasingly unable to buy those consumer items such as televisions, couches, and microwaves. The health insurance industry was going gangbusters but other parts of the economy not so much.

If disposable incomes across the country are decreasing then the economy necessarily has to shrink. I repeat the economy must shrink. One more time, if incomes across the country are decreasing then the economy must shrink. I cannot stress this point enough because people just ignore this fact or do not understand it.

Obama illustrated that in order to fix our long term growth projections then you must stop ignoring the rising cost of health care. Pure and simple, this was a necessity.

Another issue that was important not just to me, but also to an ever increasing portion of our population, was our expensive wars in the Middle East. As the years passed, many people looked at the Iraq war and asked this question, "What the hell?"

We discovered that our whole reason to attack Iraq had no basis in fact. There were no weapons of mass destruction, none, zippo, nada.

Years and years before, then President George W Bush had a big ceremony and announced "mission accomplished." This was another lie, because we were still in Iraq and American soldiers were still getting killed. The event was little more than an orchestrated publicity stunt and a photo opportunity featuring Bush in a very fashionable flight suit.

I have the utmost respect for our military men and women, but by the year 2008 I was to the point where I wanted all of our troops to come home. The cost was too great in terms of our debt and far more importantly, the cost of the lives of American soldiers. If these men and women are willing to pay the price of their life for their country then it is an inherent responsibility of our leaders to make sure the cause is just.

Early in the month of August 2008, several stories were starting to circulate through all the news channels about Iraq's budget surplus. Many had the estimate of their surplus at nearly eighty billion dollars. This was the final straw for me.

While we were accumulating massive debt, we were also rebuilding a country that had an eighty billion dollar surplus. I found this fact preposterous and dumbfounding. It took me quite some time to accept that it was even true. It was.

It was past time to get our brave men and women out of Iraq. Obama wanted to do this as well. McCain on the other hand never saw an armed confrontation he did not like.

Obama did have a problem, however. He did not have an extensive list of credentials that would suggest he could walk into the role of Commander-in-Chief very readily. McCain was a certifiable war hero.

Obama answered with a solution to the Iraq and Afghanistan wars that lent credibility to his ability to take control of our nation's military. He suggested that we should begin pulling our troops out of Iraq and focus on Afghanistan where the real problem with Al Qaeda and the Taliban lay. This path was supported by many military leaders.

While John McCain continued to pat himself on the back for the surge in Iraq which he pressed Bush for, Obama was planning what many seemed to think was the appropriate path for the future.

The people that inhabit the Middle East have lived in turmoil for centuries. It does not matter what condition we leave these countries in or whether or not we leave them with a "stable" democracy, they will still likely revert to their old ways fairly quickly.

Terrorists do not have to maintain their position. They run and hide and rebuild their operation elsewhere. They are not confined within the borders of a nation.

Obama's solution did not represent mine, but one war was better than two.

A related subject that Obama addressed with a great deal of practicality was energy independence. Energy independence is in fact a national security issue as well as an economic issue.

Would we be in the middle of two wars without our reliance on the oil obtained from that region? Possibly, but I tend to doubt that this would be true.

Our addiction to petroleum is extremely troubling. Developing alternative energies is imperative. It is the future. Ms. Palin leading chants of "drill, baby, drill" made as much sense to me as people calling for the continued use of VCR tapes or vinyl records.

America had and still has an opportunity to take a leadership role in the production of new energy technologies. This would mean higher exports and more American jobs.

Obtaining energy independence would mean our economy was not subject to the whims of oil producers in the Middle East who have their own best interests in mind and an ever present hostile opinion of the United States.

While Obama was thinking ahead, McCain and Palin were coming up with catchphrases meant to secure the votes of those dependent on the jobs provided by the petroleum industry and coal industries. Those jobs are important. Those jobs will remain. We will always need petroleum, but would it not be better if we were using petroleum from only US producers or our friendly allies?

After reviewing the opposing viewpoints on these and other issues I had reached the point where I had to admit that I was left with no choice, but to vote Democrat and for Barack Obama. The fact that I had always voted Republican was not a good enough reason to do it once again in 2008.

The McCain-Palin Implosion

There came a point during John McCain's campaign when it looked like he was just throwing spaghetti against the fridge and hoping something would stick. Unfortunately for him nothing did.

From his choice of Vice-President to calling for a halt to the campaign after the financial collapse, to assuring us that the fundamentals of the economy were sound, to his choice of Joe the plumber for Republican team mascot, and even his and Ms. Palin's incessant use of the word maverick. These gaffes and missteps would lead to his downfall.

I was also picking up on something more sinister taking place with his campaign. At a time when I felt like our country should be uniting and standing strong, McCain's camp was not only content to let his base be scared, they wanted them scared. The current environment in 2012 reveals they are still scared.

Let us look at some of his mistakes in greater detail. Before I do this, I must offer full disclosure and state that I was rather complimentary, early on, of John McCain's choice for Vice-

President in one of my opinion pieces. This article was written shortly after McCain announced his choice and when I still thought she had been properly vetted. Funny enough, this piece was used in a collaborative book with other editorials.

It is true that initially I was impressed with the bold move by the McCain camp to pick Governor Palin. She was female, attractive, a Governor and in no way represented the Washington political machine.

I would still be defending that opinion today if she had proven herself to be at all competent. She was unable to accomplish this.

Once the media finished with their vetting process we were left wondering how thorough the McCain team had been.

From suggestions that she may have abused her power as Governor to her inability to make it through an interview without leaving viewers wondering whether she could wink and chew gum at the same time, she was proving herself to be a disastrous choice.

Ah yes, the Katie Couric interview. I remember it, but I am sure Governor Palin remembers it in far more painful detail. For me I found it disturbing not only because she knew very little of the history of the Supreme Court or that the ultimate anti-abortion candidate had no idea that the Roe v Wade decision centered around privacy issues, but that she was so unsettled and unsure that she did not feel comfortable naming magazines that she read. When an interviewer asks you what you read, it should not be considered a gotcha question.

The woman who needs to write notes on her hand could one day be President of the United States. The phrase "a heartbeat away from the Presidency" was now sending shivers down the spine of intelligent, rational and often independent voters.

Yes, she drew crowds. She knew how to rile up the base of the party. The evangelical Christian conservative vote was wrapped up tight like a package. They were not going anywhere and they were always available to strike up a chant of "drill, baby, drill."

To a person, the Republican base knew what Barack Obama's middle name was, but what about the independent voters. What about those in the political center? What did they think of Sarah Palin? With every wink, with every time she uttered the word maverick, many of them were becoming nauseous. I could almost hear the political center across the county collectively saying, "Oh Hell no."

Shortly after the Palin pick, the economy crashed. The nation's largest banks were teetering on the verge of bankruptcy and a credit freeze would be necessitated. Businesses were not getting the necessary funds required to maintain their business. Mass layoffs and downsizing were on the way. Irresponsible lenders combined with irresponsible home buyers caused the mortgage crisis and the resulting rash of foreclosures. Companies in the automobile industry, with the exception of Ford, were in serious danger of closing their doors and, in fact, plants would be shut down. The failure of the auto industry would cause a chain reaction with their suppliers. Of course, Wall Street was unable to turn a blind eye to all of this and stocks plummeted.

We were suffering the worst financial crisis since the Great Depression. The proverbial sky was falling.

Mitt Romney, with his business experience and expertise in business was looking like he would have been a better choice at that moment, but I felt like we should give John McCain a chance and listen to what he had to say.

In just seven words John McCain would doom his campaign. "The fundamentals of the economy are strong." Was John McCain in over his head? Oh boy, was he ever.

As a former conservative I knew that we were going to hear about the free market fixing itself. Meanwhile hundreds of thousands and eventually millions of people would lose their jobs.

The man who could not tell us how many houses he owned was about to tell the unemployed to wait for the free market to provide the solution. He had no idea or ability to relate to the suffering that was about to ensue.

His campaign was a mess. What would he try next? John McCain thought it would be a good idea if the two men who could potentially be the next President of the United States took a break from campaigning so that they could return to Washington in an effort to try and fix the financial mess. Unbeknownst to him at the time he had just served up a soft ball to Barack Obama and Obama promptly hit it out of the park.

Obama flat out refused. What was his reasoning? To quote Barack Obama, "Part of the president's job is to deal with more than one thing at once. In my mind it's more important than ever." It is true that the people should be able to trust that the President can handle a crisis while simultaneously dealing with other major issues that the country must also deal with.

Once again Obama sounded rational and McCain seemed to be stabbing in the dark. In retrospect McCain should have stayed on the campaign trail while Barack Obama returned to Washington because McCain offered nothing of substance to the discussion or the eventual solution.

Both men would eventually vote in favor of what would become known as TARP (Troubled Asset Relief Program) or the less attractive term the "bank bailout". There is no question as to the necessity of this action despite the demonization among conservatives and the tea party. No credit or cash flow for business means no more business. By 2010 "we the people" would eventually forget that TARP was signed into law under Bush and they would eventually attribute the bailout to President Obama even though nothing could be further from the truth.

Ironically some people, like conservative commentator and game show host Ben Stein, will claim that this single act kept us from entering into another Great Depression and it was now unfair and untrue to state that President Obama kept us from another Great

Depression. For the sake of argument, let us say that Ben Stein is correct in this, and on some level he is, but it is the tea party leaders and ultra conservatives who have labeled Obama as the bailout king. In essence Obama has been left with taking all the blame and none of the credit.

Why have they labeled Obama as the bailout king? The short answer is, because they can and facts do not matter. In the 21st century there is a sizeable amount of the US population who believe that any sort of government intervention is bad and inherently evil and if they are able to put it all on Obama then it helps their cause. The American people have a tragically short memory.

Call it what you may, but this action was 100% unequivocally necessary. If it does not get done then the financial collapse would have been devastating.

Government is bad, except when it is not. Government is the problem, except when greed is rampant and uncontrolled. Government is evil, except when there is nothing else big enough or powerful enough to make a difference.

It was terribly distasteful to rescue big banks whose largesse and excesses would become legendary. It was offensive to rescue big banks when in good times, and as we would learn in bad times as well, they give billions of dollars in bonuses to their employees.

We did it not for the big banks, but for the businesses that needed the credit to maintain their business and to keep their employees working so that they could keep getting paychecks and spending their money at the grocery stores, restaurants, and clothing stores. That allows those grocery stores, restaurants, and clothing stores to keep their workers employed. If these workers are able to maintain their jobs then government would not have to provide unemployment benefits to an even greater number of people.

This is why reforming our finance system would become necessary, so that the government would not be required to do this again.

The initial price tag of seven hundred billion dollars for the bank bailout would end up reduced to fifty billion after the majority of the funds were paid back, a pretty damn cheap fix in the end to save the world's largest economy.

President George W. Bush would not do the popular thing. He would do the right thing. He could afford to do this because he was not up for re-election. For this, his legacy can at the very least read that he played a large part in keeping us from entering a second Great Depression.

For my liberal friends who are aghast that I attempting to paint W in a positive light for his efforts to stop the bleeding, let me add that he did nothing to keep the bleeding from beginning in the first place. Our present budget and debt crisis is almost entirely his burden to bear.

The financial crisis and the response from Presidential contender

John McCain provides a segue to my next point. While the incessant use of the word maverick may not have thoroughly irritated people as it did me, it provided a scary look into the future. When it came time for the tough issues did I really want a team of mavericks running the show? Did I want someone to shoot from the hip or did I want someone who would use serious thoughtful deliberation while consulting with experts before responding to the serious issues that would befall our nation? Did I want two war hawks with their fingers on the button? Hell no, I did not.

The issues that I have discussed up to this point were matters of serious concern to me.

The final point I would like to make I found to be at the best disturbing and at the worst disgusting.

Every time Governor Palin referred to a certain crowd as "real Americans", and every time one of the introducing speakers invoked Barack Obama's middle name Hussein, and every time I heard racial epithets being used in the crowd, and every sign at a McCain rally linking Obama with Osama Bin Laden or Adolf Hitler I was growing more and more incensed at the politics of division that McCain was employing seemingly to great effect.

It was them against us, only it was not about the division between Democrats and Republicans or between conservatives and liberals but rather true blue (or perhaps red would be more apropos) Americans and something else, perhaps a little scary and perhaps not even American.

While Obama's story may not be a typical American story, it was undoubtedly a great American story. We are a great nation because we are a mixing pot, not in spite of it. That someone who is to be a leader of this nation will play into the fears of one class of people against those who do not look like them is despicable.

Of course McCain and Palin will say they played no part in it, but at the very least they tolerated it and that is nearly as bad.

As recent as 2011, Governor Palin has begun invoking his middle name on camera. Many, many other conservative candidates and leaders have joined in the "fear" game. It has worked on many of us and until the American people take a stand it will continue to work.

If it has not gone far enough already, then I fear something tragic will eventually happen.

Full Disclosure – I am a Sinner

There are many things that will be cause for some to discount my opinions.

I have a sixteen year history in the gaming business. The "gaming business" is a euphemism for the casino industry. When people hear this, most want to know the best game to play in the casino, but others consider me under the influence of the Devil and tragically confused. If you are one of these people, I am not going to apologize.

I have been divorced twice, a fact that I am not proud of, nor am I ashamed of. Those marriages ended because they were supposed to end. I will never consider those marriages a mistake because they both produced children I love dearly and would not want to live without. There are many who will consider me a lost soul and unable to speak to the word of God. If you are one of these people I am not going to apologize.

If I hit my thumb with a hammer I am going to drop the F-bomb and I am probably going to scream it loud enough for my neighbors to hear.

I have abused drugs off and on in my life. I have made terrible decisions that come with being a drug user. I have told lies from time to time. I have done things I am ashamed of and there are things I needed to apologize for and did. I will not keep apologizing for them.

I have spent money foolishly and have had to declare bankruptcy. I have acted like a child when I should have acted like an adult.

Through it all I have learned and grown and never gave up. I have never said uncle.

I have suffered from anxiety and depression for the majority of my adult life. I have been on countless anti-anxiety and anti-depressant medications. I have visited counselors and psychiatrists. I could hide that part of my history, but I choose not to because I would not have been able to help the many people who have reached out to me because they were suffering the same problems and wondered how I managed to regain control of my life.

When I conquered my depression, which had become like a familiar blanket to me, I would sometimes resort to anger. It was so frustrating that I could not feel sorry for myself any longer. I would say mean things sometimes to my wife. Once again I had to learn to cope with my emotions. I still get angry, but it usually happens when I am on the phone with Comcast customer service.

My life changed when I started living by a very simple

philosophy. Stop making bad decisions and start making good decisions.

I learned that when I started to take responsibility for my own mistakes and stopped blaming others for my problems that I could make the changes necessary to take control of my life and mind.

I have a great support system which includes people that never gave up on me like my wife and mother. I worked hard learning to recognize triggers and trying out different coping mechanisms. It was exhausting at times, but well worth the effort. I accomplished all of this by the grace of God. There have been times in my life and in my marriage that I know God was looking out for me and directing my actions.

I could have just prayed and waited for God to fix my life, but I have always felt that what we obtain in this life is obtained not just by God's grace, but also through our own good and honest effort and hard work.

Today I am in a happy and successful marriage, I own my own home, I am well respected at work, my writing career continues to advance and I continue to add to my political credentials. I know I will continue to face trials because that is simply just the way it works, but I am now in a much better position to deal with those trials.

I am certainly no expert in all things spiritual. I have no degree in theology. I truly am more than a casual reader of scripture, but I am not a theologian. I do however have the desire to understand

and be inspired by the Bible. When clarification is needed I will consult with other sources so that I can make a more informed conclusion. I still decide for myself, but I have people whose opinions and knowledge I value. Valuing the positions of others is entirely different than placing blind trust in the ability of an individual to speak to God's will.

Due to the fact that I am not an expert I encourage you to check and verify everything I assert in this book.

I do not take the Bible literally in many instances. I do not respect people who pick and choose scripture to suit their needs, but do not allow that there are additional scriptures that often contradict their personal beliefs. People who place Old Testament restrictions on their lives and the lives of others, have no concept of exactly why Jesus existed.

It is not uncommon to hear a Pastor tell his congregation that the Bible is infallible, that he believes that it should be taken literally and then proceed to spend the next hour and a half explaining his interpretation of a certain passage in the Bible. This is nonsensical, yet few people sitting in the pews will see the obvious contradiction between what the pastor says and what he does.

This is the part of the book where I will begin to utilize Bible verses to support or illustrate an argument. My emphasis is always on the words of Christ. I am not a Paulian, I am a Christian.

I understand that because I do believe that the Bible contains inherent contradictions that there are those who can throw literally dozens of scriptures right back at me which would seem to argue the opposite of the case that I am trying to make. I am sure there are those who will find it necessary to shoot off e-mails and letters with their personal favorites.

Ultimately that is the point that I am trying to make, there are often two ways to look at any relevant scripture and therefore the Bible.

Often times in today's debates over scripture it is a matter of what mainstream churches teach as doctrine versus an individual's interpretation of what scripture is trying to tell or teach them.

Some churches have taught, maintained and defended their doctrine for decades, if not centuries. It is understandably not easy for them to look at something with an open mind. It is often just as difficult for their members to think that their leaders or traditional thought can be questioned. To doubt or even question usually puts people somewhere outside of their comfort zone. When it happens and a person finally says they have had enough of the hate, judgment, and condemnation that their church requires, it can be quite liberating. If you have not done so yet, try it, you just might like it.

As individuals it is our inherent right and obligation to read the Bible for ourselves. We have it within ourselves to draw our own conclusions and be able to do so without being called delusional sinners under the spell of Satan.

We should do more with our Bibles than just carry them into church where we can read a very few specific scriptures that the Pastor deems are important. Sure we can learn about a few more scriptures that are important to a Church's doctrine when we attend Bible study, but I would argue that time best spent with the Bible is after the children are put to bed, when the house is quiet and we carry that Book to our recliner or our desk and open it up and read it. We should read it word for word. Instead of relying on a Pastor's judgment on what we should or should not emphasize, let us pray for God's guidance and ask for special revelation in the moments before we begin to read.

The bestselling book in history was not meant to collect dust or be placed on a shelf near the entrance of our homes like a trophy on display meant to convey the message that we are good people and good Christians. We can best display our "goodness" if you will by fulfilling the demands of Jesus Christ.

It is important that when we read the Bible that we seek truth and do so with an open mind. We should not read it solely to prove somebody wrong or rationalize our own sins. To do this requires that we look deep within ourselves to ascertain whether we have this ability and what exactly our true intentions are.

There are many times I have been reading the Bible and I had to reread a passage again and again because the intention of a piece of particular scripture is often unclear or difficult to understand.

When I read the words of Jesus Christ however, I am never

confused. I rarely wonder what his true message is or what the truth is. Everything is clear and I am secure in the knowledge that I am learning a true path and receiving the ultimate guidance. When I read the words of the Apostles and their instructions that would become the foundation for an organized church, I sometimes get confused and things become unclear.

Sometimes I have the profound feeling that our leaders whether they be in business, government or even our church are scared to death when their workers, constituents, or parishioners start to think for themselves. Thinking tends to lead to organizing and they cannot have that.

One man dared to disagree with the Roman Catholic Church, Martin Luther, and changed the dynamic of Christianity forever. It is hard to control people who do not just blindly follow and who would rather not accept the status quo, but instead question and lead with a new truth and a new promise.

The New Testament teaches us in many ways that the path to Heaven is accepting Jesus Christ as our Savior and asking forgiveness of our sins. It says this throughout the New Testament.

It does not say that I have to believe that the world was created in six 24 hour periods or that the world is six thousand years old.

It does not say that I have to tell every gay person that I meet that they are an abomination in the eyes of God and that they must be suffering from a sickness, deserve no special protection under the law and are bound for a fiery damnation in Hell.

It does not say that I have to be of the understanding that every natural disaster is God's judgment on us. That is the Old Testament God. The New Testament tells us that Jesus came so that there would be a new way. Many pastors ignore this fact.

The great demagogue Pat Robertson gets far more press when he blames hurricanes and earthquakes on God's wrath than when he talks about the promise of God's love.

If these were requirements for being a Christian then I could not be and would not be a Christian.

It is "end times" tele-celebrities such as Jack Van Impe and the others who personally made a great deal of money by scaring the crap out of people before the year 2000 which at one time contributed to me walking away from the church and God.

At that time I failed to recognize that the church and God are not the same. God is not responsible for the utter failings and greed of some of the leaders of the Church.

Ultimately it would not be a church leader that would bring me back, but rather the compassionate and hopeful words of Christ found in the Bible and the persistent, but gentle urging of my wife. I will always wonder what the true growth of the church could be if the focus were not on the manufactured fear utilized to some effect by evangelical leaders, but rather the hope and compassion that Jesus not only offers but guarantees.

I repeat, it says that I should accept Jesus Christ as my savior and ask forgiveness for my sins. Because this is what it says I can say that I am a Christian. Not perfect, not a saint, still searching for truth, but a Christian nonetheless.

And I will not apologize for this.

Rationalize This

In this chapter I would like to illustrate what I am referring to when I claim that it is ludicrous to suggest that the Bible is not subject to interpretation. More to the point though, is that if you agree that some passages are subject to interpretation then you cannot really say another passage must be taken literally as written.

In the gospels we learn through a speech given by Jesus to his disciples on the Mount of Olives what the last days of the world will be like and how to know when to look for Jesus' return. I will quote from Luke:

> 7 "Teacher," they asked, "when will these things happen? And what will be the sign that they are about to take place?"
>
> 8 He replied: "Watch out that you are not deceived. For many will come in my name, claiming, 'I am he,' and, 'The time is near.' Do not follow them. 9 When you hear of wars and uprisings, do not be frightened. These things must happen first, but the end will not come right away."

¹⁰ Then he said to them: "Nation will rise against nation, and kingdom against kingdom. ¹¹ There will be great earthquakes, famines and pestilences in various places, and fearful events and great signs from heaven.

¹² "But before all this, they will seize you and persecute you. They will hand you over to synagogues and put you in prison, and you will be brought before kings and governors, and all on account of my name. ¹³ And so you will bear testimony to me. ¹⁴ But make up your mind not to worry beforehand how you will defend yourselves. ¹⁵ For I will give you words and wisdom that none of your adversaries will be able to resist or contradict. ¹⁶ You will be betrayed even by parents, brothers and sisters, relatives and friends, and they will put some of you to death. ¹⁷ Everyone will hate you because of me. ¹⁸ But not a hair of your head will perish. ¹⁹ Stand firm, and you will win life.

²⁰ "When you see Jerusalem being surrounded by armies, you will know that its desolation is near. ²¹ Then let those who are in Judea flee to the mountains, let those in the city get out, and let those in the country not enter the city. ²² For this is the time of punishment in fulfillment of all that has been written. ²³ How dreadful it will be in those days for pregnant women and nursing mothers! There will be great distress in the land and wrath against this people. ²⁴ They will fall by the sword and will be taken as prisoners to all

the nations. Jerusalem will be trampled on by the Gentiles until the times of the Gentiles are fulfilled.

[25] "There will be signs in the sun, moon and stars. On the earth, nations will be in anguish and perplexity at the roaring and tossing of the sea. [26] People will faint from terror, apprehensive of what is coming on the world, for the heavenly bodies will be shaken. [27] At that time they will see the Son of Man coming in a cloud with power and great glory. [28] When these things begin to take place, stand up and lift up your heads, because your redemption is drawing near."

[29] He told them this parable: "Look at the fig tree and all the trees. [30] When they sprout leaves, you can see for yourselves and know that summer is near. [31] Even so, when you see these things happening, you know that the kingdom of God is near.

[32] "Truly I tell you, this generation will certainly not pass away until all these things have happened. (Luke 21:7-32 NIV)

Please pay special attention to Luke 21:32. Taken literally, this passage would suggest that the Apostle's generation would not die before the return of Christ. There is no other way to take it, if you want a literal interpretation. So if you must take it literally then the implication is that Christianity is done and is based on a false premise.

I and everyone else who are Christians allow that it is subject to interpretation. The most common and accepted interpretation is that Jesus was referring not to a generation as we are familiar with, but rather the entire existence of the Jewish people.

There are some theorists who are labeled as preterists who take passages such as this so literally that they proclaim that all the prophecies concerning Christ's return have already occurred and had occurred by 70 AD.

There are other scriptures that today's evangelical churches take exception to. Take for instance the ability of a woman to Pastor a church or even to teach others about the word of God.

Let us reference Paul's letter to Timothy:

> "[11] A woman should learn in quietness and full submission. [12] I do not permit a woman to teach or to assume authority over a man; she must be quiet. [13] For Adam was formed first, then Eve. [14] And Adam was not the one deceived; it was the woman who was deceived and became a sinner. [15] But women will be saved through childbearing—if they continue in faith, love and holiness with propriety." (Timothy 2:11-15 NIV)

Paul reveals the same principles in his first Epistle to the Corinthians:

> "[34] Women should remain silent in the churches. They are not allowed to speak, but must be in submission, as the law says. [35] If they want to inquire about something, they

should ask their own husbands at home; for it is disgraceful for a woman to speak in the church." (Corinthians 14:34-35 NIV)

If we take these passages literally then women have no business being on the altar of a church singing, let alone taking a leadership role in a church. We can take it even further and suggest that Sarah Palin had no business aspiring to the second highest office in the land or even her previous role as mayor of Wasilla Alaska.

There are more incredulous passages that deal with such things as the concept that women should not cut their hair and that slaves should obey their masters. A fact that slave owners in the pre-civil war era used to justify their treatment of their slaves and to justify their fight to keep and maintain slaves.

Now if we accept that these passages must be interpreted in some other way than how it is written why therefore must we take very literally the story of creation and the fact it was done in six 24 hour periods before God's obligatory resting day. And if we do not think that we have to take the 6-24 time frame literally does it necessarily suggest that we are lesser Christians or even that we are wrong?

On two occasions and from two different people I have gotten a very similar response when I asked whether or not it was necessary to believe in the 6-24 time frame to be a Christian. They both hesitated and said no, but added, if you can believe it then your experience as a Christian will be that much richer and your faith will be stronger.

To which I said, actually "I believe that God could do it in the blink of an eye, in a millisecond. Since you say it took him 144 hours is my faith actually much, much more stronger than yours?"

After considerable hemming and hawing and increased flow of blood to the face I received answers that were non-sensical and had the feeling of being contrived.

Many people will use the argument, especially concerning the role of women in church, that you have to consider the time and context in which the scriptures were written. They have no problem suggesting that since times have changed and people and their knowledge about how things work has grown, then surely God would not hold today's churches to the same procedural rules that they did back then.

Would it be that much of a stretch to assert that since the Old Testament was written as early as 1400 years before Christ, that it was written in a way that people of that time could understand. People had no concept of evolution and it would be a few millennia before anyone could conceive of the "big bang theory". That humans evolve is indisputable. The changes in the human body and mind that have occurred over even just the last one hundred years are significant.

I do believe that God created all things under the heavens and on the earth. I just do not believe it occurred in 6-24 hour days, nor do I believe that the world is only 6000 years old. Yet there are those who will make exceptions to certain scriptures such as the women's role in churches, but insist that I absolutely positively must take the creation story as written verbatim and it must be taken literally and any interpretation otherwise is heresy. I disagree and I could not disagree more vehemently. If this is true I better start hearing more people shouting, "Sit down lady. Know your place." when I visit churches.

Furthermore, if I must consider the context and time when a scripture was written when considering how it may or may not apply today, why can I not take the stance that the writers of the New Testament knew absolutely nothing about sexual orientation and therefore anything they write about homosexuality is no longer applicable? The concept of sexual orientation was not even defined or discussed until the 1800's.

You will hear some offer evidence within the Bible to suggest that these and other scriptures are not to be taken literally. Would this not be evidence of contradictions in the Bible? A thought that some would consider being heretical since the Bible is supposed to represent absolute truth created through the breath of God and the guidance of the Holy Spirit, which is difficult if there are contradictory assertions.

The New Testament was put together by men, like you and me, over three hundred years after Jesus died. These men had a personal bias that they used to decide what writings and letters would be included in the New Testament. Teachings attributed to certain Apostles and early church leaders would be included and teachings from other Apostles would be left out.

More to the point of this entire book is this, people can disagree on what the Bible says and it is okay. One is not more Christian than the other. One is not more evil than the other. In fact neither side has to be evil.

There are literally hundreds of different types of churches in the United States, all with different philosophies and teaching different doctrines. Many are led by thoughtful, well read, well-educated leaders who have studied the Bible for years and yet have come to many different conclusions. None can be proven wrong and none can be proven right. None have the authority of God and all are subject to the limitations of being human and possess the ability to make mistakes.

Yet God does make this one singular promise to all of us, "If you declare with your mouth, "Jesus is Lord," and believe in your heart that God raised him from the dead, you will be saved." (Romans 10:9 NIV)

There are no exceptions discussed and no clarification needed. This applies to all including adulterers, liars, drunkards, thieves and even those who are gay or lesbian and the people who choose to defend them.

When Christians Attack

As a Republican for most of my life and one that was not a
Republican for religious or moral reasons I had been unaware of
the ruthlessness with which Evangelical Christian conservatives
malign Democrats and their ideals.

I knew there were many during the Clinton administration that
suspected he was the anti-Christ, but honestly I did not think they
were serious. I realize now that they were. Now that President
Clinton has assumed the traditional activities of a former President
we can say with a great degree of certainty that they were wrong.

Do members of the Christian right ever retract their prior
statements? No, they just wait until the next Democratic
Presidential candidate comes along and slap the anti-Christ label
on him in an effort to scare people into voting for another Wall
Street owned Republican and against their own best interests. It
really is a remarkably effective strategy.

I truly believe that any Democratic President in the immediate
future will be labeled as the anti-Christ. Of course, a black man
with the middle name of Hussein is an easy target, much more so

than a President with the middle name of Jefferson.

Whether it is the fire and brimstone pastor warning that you must toe the Christian line or face a fiery damnation in hell or the Tea Party leader warning against the evil fascist Barack Hussein Obama, I have always had difficulty being swayed by people who tried to use fear to motivate me in one direction over another.

They do this because fear works with some people. I must admit that I do have a lesser opinion of those who succumb to this tactic. I personally believe it is a sign of weakness in one's character. Put another way fear works best on the weak, naïve, ignorant and vulnerable.

Many will argue and argue correctly that fear is often times a successful survival mechanism that triggers the flight or fight reaction. This being true, I would also like to point out that Democrats are not wielding axes and beating down doors in an effort to bludgeon conservatives in their sleep.

Shortly before the 2008 elections my wife told me that an acquaintance of ours had informed her that if Barack Obama were elected President that "it will be bad."

I kept waiting to be filled in on why "it will be bad," but when there was no further indication from my wife that there was anything else she cared to add I went ahead and asked, "why will it be bad?"

My wife responded, "I don't know. She didn't say."

That was when it hit me. It was another one of those ominous warnings. It was as if she had said it with a wink and no explanation was necessary. Obama likes gay people and he is pro-choice therefore bad things are going to happen to our country.

To these people I suggest how ironic it is that under the pro-choice Clinton administration we had tremendous economic growth and a failed attempt at bringing down the World Trade Center, yet under the pro-life candidate George W Bush we had the worst recession since the Great Depression, terrorists really did bring down the World Trade Center, two wars and Hurricane Katrina. So much for God blessing the country when we choose a pro-life candidate.

We all have the time to do what it takes to discover the truth. We have time to look at the facts and evaluate exactly what is going on in this country. It is imperative that we do this if we are going to call ourselves good citizens. What people think sometimes has little to do with reality.

People have placed real faith in a certain group of politicians and "news" celebrulists and rely on only those people to discern the truth and let them know what they should think. They never ask the question, "What if they are wrong?"

I used to be a Republican, but now I am a Democrat because I asked the question, "What if they are wrong?" I then proceeded to analyze the numbers and historical data. My eventual conclusion was that they were in fact wrong. They were terribly wrong.

What does it take to be able to ask that question? It takes an open mind, perhaps some curiosity, and the ability to accept that you can make a mistake. Most people have a very hard time admitting when they are wrong.

There are many, many people who do not possess these necessary ingredients. What would motivate people to take a longer look at that question? One possibility is the belief that it is important to the future of our nation and the understanding that it is nearly impossible to make a good decision when you do not use numbers that have no basis in fact.

Whoever figures out how to separate Republican voters from Fox News long enough to hear the other side of the story could become a very, very highly valued and well paid political operative.

At the core of my beliefs is this; a politician that must use fear to motivate me instead of appealing to my intellect must have a fundamental problem with their policy.

In the run up to the 2008 election the non-inclusive churches, as I prefer to call them, had begun a process of divisiveness. They were dividing their congregations down the middle and just like in Congress there would be no attempt to reach across the aisle.

It seemed as if there was now an 11th Commandment. In addition to admonitions such as thou shall not kill and thou shall not steal we were now faced with "thou shall not vote Democrat." The penalties for violating the 11th Commandment were more sinister than for the first ten. You can be forgiven for committing murder, but not for voting Democrat. This idea is reinforced every time a pastor asks, "How can you call yourself a Christian if...?"

It is not just that they give the impression that there is a righteous party and an unrighteous party, but rather a righteous party and an evil sinister party that will kill your babies, granny, and handicapped people. There is a righteous party and then there is the one that worships Lenin, Stalin, and Hitler and kneels at the altar of socialism. There is a righteous party and then there is the one who has no regard for the Constitution, is ashamed of America and wants to burn the flag. I could go on and on with this game, but I think you get the picture.

We have talked about the lies perpetrated by politicians and the media, but what about the churches and the leaders of those churches. The Sunday before Election Day many churches distributed literature as people were leaving the service. The literature that I am familiar with and that was distributed at the church I was attending at the time offered an extremely biased and deceptive take on the positions of each Presidential candidate on certain moral issues.

I will speak about just one of the false claims (lies) offered in the literature. The flyer suggested that Barack Obama had voted for legislation which called for Kindergarten students to be taught sex education. An incredulous statement, yet the masses did not ask if it was really true. Instead they said, "Really? That is horrible. That is disgusting."

Why should they question the validity of this statement? Their church and their pastor had not only approved the message, but made sure it was disseminated to their members.

Of course the problem with this is that it was patently, undeniably false. It was a lie. It was a lie perpetrated by the church and by the pastor.

President Obama had voted for legislation that called for our youngest students to learn how to react if faced with a sexual predator. "Good touch, bad touch" type of stuff. That sounds reasonable and unfortunately, in this day and age, it seems to be necessary.

This is the perfect example of the tactics of Christian fundamentalists. They paint something in the worst possible light to get the reaction they want, but they put a little truth in their statements to cover their butt and perhaps ease their conscious. The legislation did deal with sex in the form of sexual predators and it did deal with education in that it would be taught in schools.

The perpetrators of this lie realize that telling someone that a candidate believes in sex education for kindergartners is far scarier than telling someone that a candidate believes that kindergartners should be taught how to identify sexual predators and how to react if they have to deal with a sexual predator.

A similar example is the conservative attempt to paint the leader of the Democratic Party as Hitler. The majority of people who make this comparison cannot tell you what policies a particular politician has that are similar to Hitler's or even if they, in fact had any similar policy ideas. The important thing in their opinion is that they feel this person is just as bad as Hitler.

In the end the only thing that people think about when they think of Hitler is that he killed millions of people in gas chambers and in firing squads. Is it really fair to compare anyone to Hitler? Any comparison to Hitler without discussing specifics is too inflammatory.

Ultimately the pushing of a political agenda is in direct violation of Federal law if a church is to continue their tax exempt status. Violating the law of the land is in direct violation of scripture.

There is evidence to suggest that non-conforming to the law of the state is acceptable when it goes against God's will, but I really do not think that a law requiring that a Church not endorse a specific political candidate or political party in order to keep a tax-exempt status would be abhorrent to God.

We learn in Romans;

> "[1] Let everyone be subject to the governing authorities, for there is no authority except that which God has established. The authorities that exist have been established by God. [2] Consequently, whoever rebels against the authority is rebelling against what God has instituted, and those who do so will bring judgment on themselves. [3] For rulers hold no terror for those who do right, but for those who do wrong. Do you want to be free from fear of the one in

authority? Then do what is right and you will be commended. [4] For the one in authority is God's servant for your good. But if you do wrong, be afraid, for rulers do not bear the sword for no reason. They are God's servants, agents of wrath to bring punishment on the wrongdoer. [5] Therefore, it is necessary to submit to the authorities, not only because of possible punishment but also as a matter of conscience." (Romans 13:1-5 NIV)

We receive the same message in Peter;

"13 Submit yourselves for the Lord's sake to every human authority: whether to the emperor, as the supreme authority, 14 or to governors, who are sent by him to punish those who do wrong and to commend those who do right. 15 For it is God's will that by doing good you should silence the ignorant talk of foolish people. 16 Live as free people, but do not use your freedom as a cover-up for evil; live as God's slaves. 17 Show proper respect to everyone, love the family of believers, fear God, honor the emperor." (Peter 2:13-17 NIV)

The idea of the separation of Church and State does not just apply to government staying out of the churches business; it also applies to churches staying out of the government's business.

If you will allow me to engage in a little hyperbole, if you are a fundamentalist and you believe the Bible must be taken literally then it is pretty clear that Barack Obama was placed at the head of the government by God.

It is equally clear that every Republican in the Congress and Senate who is trying desperately to keep legislation proposed by the Obama administration from being passed and sent to Obama's desk to be signed is doing so in opposition of God's will. That statement was a lot of hyperbole.

I guess we should just overlook the scripture I just cited just as certain pastors do. These were just two scriptures that you will not hear discussed in church on Sunday.

Good Christian, Bad Christian

In my world I hear a great deal about good Christians and what it takes to be a good Christian. It has gotten to the point where I am actually very tired of hearing the words "good Christian."

What does it mean exactly? Do we have to refer to Christians as good and bad? Can we not just be Christians?

In an effort to clear up any misconceptions and further illuminate what it takes to be a top tier Christian I would like to propose a rating system.

**** 4 Star Christians: These are the people that are the holiest of the holy. These people are firmly ingrained in the doctrine of their church. Doctrine supersedes scripture.

At the same time that they attack the Catholic Church for believing that the Pope has a direct link to God and is not capable of making a mistake concerning scripture or the message of God, 4 Stars believe their pastor incapable of misleading or misinterpreting the Bible. His message is above question on all matters and anyone who does question the pastor is on the path to spiritual destruction.

4 Stars have reached such a high level in their holiness that they are entitled and in fact obligated to judge others for their sins. They can determine who is going to hell and must scare the crap out of everyone so that they will see the light. It worked for them, why would it not work for everyone else. They expend a great deal of energy and take great pride in condemning people who gamble, drink and drop the occasional "F bomb" to a fiery eternity in Hell.

They are very efficient people who can remember the scriptures the Pastor gives them in Sunday's services and therefore have no need to read the Bible on their own. The Pastor has done their work for them.

They love everyone and embrace all children of God except for those children of God who do not go to their church, have caught "the gay", just about everyone from California, and sometimes even people who look a little different than themselves. They will be more than happy to explain their reasoning as long as it is after The Ellen Degeneres Show.

They are Republican to a fault. They embrace the term Constitutional conservative, but really have no idea what that means. They believe in the sanctity of the Constitution except for certain parts. They have a real problem with the Amendment that calls for a separation of Church and State. They get upset that their religion has little influence over the government and has restricted access to public schools.

They believe that our founders envisioned a Christian based government, and have apparently forgotten that many of their Christian ancestors came to North America to escape religious persecution and to be able to worship how they please. They have failed to ask the question, if they envisioned a Christian based government then why did they not just create a Christian based government?

*** <u>3 Star Christians</u>: The 3 stars are much like the 4 stars. They essentially believe the same thing except they only go to church on Christmas, Easter and when their parents come to visit. They own a Bible but probably cannot tell you where it is located. They know it is okay to hate gay people because of the whole Sodom and Gomorrah thing.

These Christians know the passage, "where 2 or 3 are gathered in my name" thing like the palm of their hand and use it as often as necessary to justify not going to Church especially during football season.

** <u>2 Star Christians</u>: This particular breed of Christian cannot tell you the last time they were in a church. More than likely if it was recent it was because their cousin was getting married. They know they are Christian because their mother and father told them they were. Many maintain their allegiance to the label Christian because they do not want to end up in Hell. Besides what else are they going to be since Jews are greedy and all Muslim's kill people?

Often times they are good hard working people. They wonder if it is bad when they go to a bar and drink a couple after work, but it does not trouble them enough to go straight home. They go about their day with the understanding that if they cheat on their spouse that they will be okay if they do not die before they can ask for forgiveness or even better, have time to get serious about church going.

*1 Star Christians: These people are very, very confused. These are the bad Christians. As hard as they might try and as much as their pastor tells them they should, they find it difficult to hate people or to judge them. They remember somewhere along the line learning that we are all God's children and when Jesus talked about the whole "judge not lest ye be judged" thing, they actually believe he meant it.

When faced with indisputable evidence that today's teenagers who are struggling with their sexual orientation are being bullied and leading some of them to kill themselves, 1-stars would find it difficult to tell anyone in the same situation that they are an abomination in God's eyes and that the wages of sin is death. This is especially difficult for them since we all sin every day.

When their pastor tells them that he knows it is hard to do this, but that you must because it is showing that you truly love them and care for them, they start looking for another church or more likely stay home. It is implied that their salvation depends on them not being gay which, of course to anyone who knows the teachings of Jesus, could not be further from the truth.

They tend to concentrate on the good in the world and not the bad. They focus on the man first and worry about the sin when they have that person's attention and trust.

When tragedy strikes they marvel at the heroism and goodness in people who supported the victims and decide not to blame destruction on God's wrath for one particular sin or another.

When they wonder "what would Jesus do" they may ask another person, but they will also open up the Bible so they can discover what Jesus actually did. When they learn that he sat down with the sinners a 1 star Christian questions the validity of certain church doctrines which exclude individuals or groups of people from being welcome in their church.

Many believe that God created the Heavens and the earth, but that perhaps it was not necessarily done in six 24 hour periods. Many are confused as to why they have to believe in such a strict time frame and are even more hesitant to believe the earth is only 6000 years old. The mountain of scientific evidence against this theory would make Mt. Everest look like Bunker Hill.

They recognize that traditional churches uses science when it supports their dogma, but persecute the scientist when it goes against their dogma.

Copernicus and Galileo suffered the persecution of the church when they dared to support the heretical theory that the earth revolved around the sun. Of course we know how that turned out.

Columbus was warned by leaders of the church that he would fall off the edge of the earth on his voyage due to his lack of faith and respect for church leaders who claimed that the earth was flat.

Today's Christians that disagree with the six 24 hour time frame for creation are attacked and persecuted as well. They show a lesser faith. They certainly are not good Christians. They are confused. The devil has twisted their minds. They are ignorant, weak and all too easily influenced by facts and evidence.

Many 1 stars believe in the separation of Church and State. They do not understand why the government should be teaching their children what they can and should be learning at home.

As for myself I would fall into the 1-star category or the bad Christian category. I admit I paint a pretty harsh and sarcastic picture of certain members of the Christian faith. Perhaps we are all just trying to do the right thing and we have the best intentions, but we cannot all be right.

The fact is that there is a certain segment of the population that rejects Christianity because they see its members as I have just described them. They do not feel welcome. They see believing in an earth that is six thousand years old as a requirement to being a Christian. They see intolerance against the homosexual community as being a requirement and yes, more and more, some think that being a Republican is a requirement to being a Christian. Since they reject these ideas or concepts then they reject the Christian faith. They will never walk into a church and to me this is devastating.

Why do they feel this way? It boils down to the fact that the Christian Churches that make the headlines are churches such as the bigoted Westboro Baptist Church which operates the website godhatesfags.com and pickets outside of soldiers funerals. They hear Pat Robertson blaming Hurricane Katrina or the devastating earthquake in Haiti on the sins of the people or the sins of their ancestors. They see the gun toting Pastor Terry Jones of the ironically named Dove World Outreach Center threatening to create an uproar because he wanted to burn the Koran. They see case after case of great hypocrisy by some leaders of the church.

What they do not see or realize is that the majority of Christians are good people, people that would give you the shirt off of their back.

It is unfortunate, but in today's world being bad gets you far more exposure than being good.

The Devil is in the Details

This book is not about painting Republicans as evil and Democrats as good. There are good Republicans and bad Republicans and the same goes for Democrats. I believe that neither party is righteous. When you embrace one party as righteous because of their position on one or two particular policies then one places themselves in a position where they must define all of the party's policies as righteous. Sometimes this takes a great dealing of rationalizing on the behalf of Christians.

There are parts of the Republican platform that many fundamentalists will say are righteous. The most obvious, most righteous policy is their anti-abortion stance. Anti-gay rights legislation is a close second.

Unfortunately for the rest of us these are the only two "righteous" policies that many conservatives advocate for.

When you talk about questionable policies in the Republican Party you must talk about their support for the death penalty, defense of torture (waterboarding), their zeal for war, their rejection of anti-poverty programs, their persistent and relentless support for the wealthy through tax cuts, their opposition to universal access to health care, their fervent anti-illegal immigrant stance, and their utter lack of concern for the environment.

They cannot point to anything Jesus Christ said to support their policy positions on these issues. They must look to the Old Testament or the teachings and letters of later Christians.

When performing the research for the following chapters, I must admit that I found much more evidence to support a progressive or liberal stance on social or economic issues than I could have ever dreamed.

For many, what follows will be an eye-opening experience. It will be a relief for some that have grown up in a Christian home, but had a different outlook on people and life than their parents or pastor, to find out that there really is nothing wrong with them.

If your instincts keep telling you that someone or something is totally screwed up when people think that intolerance, greed, lack of compassion, hate and inhumane murder and treatment of other men regardless of their sins is congruent with Christ's message then read closely the following chapters.

I have made every effort to cite New Testament evidence to support my assertions, but I did make exception on occasion to prove a point or when it just made sense due to little discussion relating to a specific policy in the New Testament.

I reserve the right to cite Old Testament scripture, because fundamentalists use the Old Testament often when it suits their needs.

On the Death Penalty

I personally cannot imagine losing a child via the hands of another person without wanting that person to suffer the same fate.

In today's society we are well aware of the most heinous acts committed by both insane and sane alike. It is difficult to fathom the height of evil that some are able to attain. It is fairly easy to think that there are many in our prisons today who have committed crimes worthy of death.

Those in favor of the death penalty often point to Hammurabi's Code which can first be found in the Bible in Exodus;

> 23 But if there is serious injury, you are to take life for life, 24 eye for eye, tooth for tooth, hand for hand, foot for foot, 25 burn for burn, wound for wound, bruise for bruise.
>
> (Exodus 21:23-25 NIV)

This for obvious reasons would seem to support the right of our governments to impose the death penalty in severe cases.

Those against the death penalty often cite scripture from the New Testament such as these words found in Matthew;

> 39 But I tell you, do not resist an evil person. If anyone slaps

you on the right cheek, turn to them the other cheek also. (Matthew 5:39 NIV)

Many of us learned this when we were little. Many of us found this a bit difficult to stomach.

If you place Matthew 5:39 in context you realize that the author was both referencing Hammurabi's code and invalidating it at the same time.

[38] "You have heard that it was said, 'Eye for eye, and tooth for tooth.' [39] But I tell you, do not resist an evil person. If anyone slaps you on the right cheek, turn to them the other cheek also. [40] And if anyone wants to sue you and take your shirt, hand over your coat as well. [41] If anyone forces you to go one mile, go with them two miles. [42] Give to the one who asks you, and do not turn away from the one who wants to borrow from you.

[43] "You have heard that it was said, 'Love your neighbor and hate your enemy.' [44] But I tell you, love your enemies and pray for those who persecute you, [45] that you may be children of your Father in heaven. He causes his sun to rise on the evil and the good, and sends rain on the righteous and the unrighteous. [46] If you love those who love you, what reward will you get? Are not even the tax collectors doing that? [47] And if you greet only your own people, what are you doing more than others? Do not even pagans do that? [48] Be perfect, therefore, as your heavenly Father is

perfect. (Matthew 5:38-48 NIV)

As a Christian I find it difficult to understand why references in the Old Testament would take priority over what Jesus himself taught us. In my personal beliefs the words of Jesus supersedes anything said by anyone in the Old Testament. Jesus came to show us a new way. He was the new sheriff in town and he was not going to be hanging anyone any time soon.

There is one additional point that we must consider. While our legal system is superior to anything else out there, it is still flawed. Mistakes happen when men are involved. With the advent of DNA evidence we have seen several people found innocent and released from death row based upon re-examination of the evidence. These are people who often were slated to be executed by the state.

It seems likely that our government has sponsored, authorized and performed the execution of innocent individuals. When you put it another way as in, our government has killed or murdered innocent Americans it makes many a bit queasy.

With evidence such as this I think we must decide if this risk is necessary and if it provides enough of a disincentive for people to commit the most heinous of crimes. It is difficult to quantify the effectiveness of the death penalty in preventing crimes. Life behind bars would seem to many to be a sufficient disincentive. If we can acknowledge that mistakes do happen, perhaps we can make the leap that the death penalty should, at the very least, be overhauled within the courts or simply abolished by state legislators.

There are many issues which are just not easy to reconcile when we are faced with what Christ commands us to do on one hand and how we feel as living, thinking human beings faced with living in an imperfect world on the other hand. The death penalty is one such issue.

It is okay not to know for sure. One does not have to have everything figured out and doing the right thing often involves personal struggle. I question anybody who feels or implies that they know the proper opinion a Christian is supposed to hold in all instances.

There have been cases when the parent of a child who has been murdered decides to advocate against the death penalty in the case of the very person who murdered their children.

I cannot wrap my head around how a parent comes to this decision. Perhaps I would make the same decision, but I do not dare commit to anything for certain. I do not know the level of grace a person must feel to be able to advocate for the murderer of their child. As a loving and proud father of five I cannot imagine the depth of pain and anger that must accompany the news of the death of your child. I can certainly understand the impulse for a parent to avenge the murder of a child.

There are certain individuals such as Oklahoma City bomber Timothy McVeigh who by their own admission commited a crime against children and dozens of other people.

McVeigh was sentenced to death. I cried no tears that day. I had a sense that justice had been performed. That justice however, was provided by man. Man did not turn the other cheek, man took a life for the many lives that he took, but should not the ultimate judgment be His and only His?

During one of the early Republican debates in 2011, then Presidential Candidate Rick Perry had this to say about the death penalty and the large number of executions he has authorized, "In the state of Texas, if you come into our state and you kill one of our children, you kill a police officer, you're involved with another crime and you kill one of our citizens, you will face the ultimate justice in the state of Texas, and that is you will be executed."

The crowd's response was raucous and enthusiastic. Even people who support the death penalty were a little disturbed by this reaction. Even people who agreed with the statement found the crowd reaction disturbing. There was a sense that any response when you are talking about government mandated murder of an American citizen should at least be thoughtful and more dignified. The "lynch mob" mentality on display at that particular debate and on that particular night was a little unsettling and certainly not Christ-like or righteous.

On Torture

You can use many of the same arguments in reference to torture that you do concerning the death penalty. Torture is seen throughout the Bible being perpetrated against the godly and never by the godly. There is little to reference in the Bible that we can use to justify or not justify torture.

The Bible does give government the authority to punish those who do wrong. There is nothing however, to suggest that they can use any means necessary. To suggest that Christ would have or could have advocated for torture seems a bit absurd.

If the people who authorized the torture on the prisoners located at Guantanamo Bay would have asked themselves, "What would Jesus do?" their answer would not have been, "We've got to water board him."

While we abhor the use of torture by other nations and other governments it is reasonable to suggest that we should hold ourselves to a higher standard.

I consider my country, the United States to be the greatest nation on the planet. This belief to me does not mean we can do whatever we want and justify it because we are the greatest. Rather we are the greatest because we do what is right without any consideration of what everyone else is doing. We should set the bar for protecting the basic fundamental rights of all people.

Dignity can sometimes be lacking in a world where there is video evidence of our soldiers urinating on dead Taliban fighters. We must face the realization that there are many of us who do not act in a dignified manner. Using the excuse "they do worse to our soldiers" is representative of an eighth grade, barbaric mentality and is not indicative of a nation that holds itself to a higher standard.

In case I have not presented a sufficient argument for you, perhaps you will listen to someone who had to endure torture for several years at the hands of the North Vietnamese, Senator and former Republican Presidential candidate John McCain, "If we inflict this cruel and inhumane treatment, the cruel actions of a few darken the reputation of our country in the eyes of millions. American values should win against all others in any war of ideas, and we can't let prisoner abuse tarnish our image."

I will Let John McCain have the final word on this subject.

On War

War is another subject that regardless of which side a particular person supports, you can rest assured that they will have a strong opinion.

Supporters of war and those who seek to justify war most often cite Old Testament scripture. Pacifists or people who abhor war generally cite New Testament scripture.

Jesus is often referred to as the Prince of Peace. The following scripture supports this viewpoint;

> [17] Do not repay anyone evil for evil. Be careful to do what is right in the eyes of everyone. [18] If it is possible, as far as it depends on you, live at peace with everyone. [19] Do not take revenge, my dear friends, but leave room for God's wrath, for it is written: "It is mine to avenge; I will repay," says the Lord. [20] On the contrary:
>
> "If your enemy is hungry, feed him; if he is thirsty, give him something to drink. In doing this, you will heap burning coals on his head."
>
> [21] Do not be overcome by evil, but overcome evil with good.

(Romans 12:17-21 NIV)

Personally I do believe that there are just and unjust wars or perhaps necessary and unnecessary wars.

Many on the political left, including myself, will assert that war should be a last resort. All possible means of diplomacy or sanctions should be used to create a solution where war is not necessary. Often times the knowledge that a nation is willing to go to war is enough to prevent the actual war.

A nation should never go to war for financial gain or for the acquisition of natural resources such as oil. A nation should never go to war to expand their borders. A nation should never go to war for political reasons or continue that war because it will play well politically for the party in power.

There is great cost associated with war. The most devastating cost is the loss of human life. In war, it is not simply the soldier who pays with their life, it is often innocent civilians. These civilians who die are considered necessary collateral damage. While I do believe the United States, in most instances, makes every effort to limit the loss of innocent human life, it is still inevitable and certainly unfortunate.

The sin for me is not in a willingness to go to war, but rather in an eagerness to go to war. Was Iraq a just war or a necessary war? In retrospect the answer appears to be that entering into a war with Iraq was unwarranted. There was a far better case for the Afghanistan war, but still the question is, was even that war really necessary?

Should we enter a war when we do not have a clear definition of what victory looks like? I think this is what dismays most people. A considerable amount of time has passed since the war began and people are starting to wonder what exactly we are doing over there. Meanwhile our brave men and women are continuing to die.

At the time of this writing, there are Republicans who seek to begin hostilities with Iran and with North Korea. They want to do this while we are still knee deep in Afghanistan.

In May of 2012, on the anniversary of Osama Bin Laden's death, President Obama paid a visit to Afghanistan and announced that by the end of 2014 the troop withdrawal from Afghanistan will be complete.

It has been an incredibly long journey for our country. Our military families and their lives have been dramatically changed. The time has come and I am grateful that our Commander-in-Chief has taken action to complete the transition from a nation always at war to a nation that enters into conflict only when undeniably necessary.

At some point we have to consider if, after ten years of fighting two wars in Iraq and Afghanistan that our national security may be jeopardized.

Our enemies know the tremendous financial devastation these wars have had on our economy. They know the loss of life that we have suffered. Because of these two factors they also know the unwillingness of the American people to engage in or support another war.

Our enemies must sense that they have much more latitude in the games that they play and the threats that they make simply because we are much more hesitant to go to war today than we were ten years ago. This is not a good situation for the United States.

Certainly our enemies fully realize that there is a line they can cross in which the United States would have to act, but the realization has also set in that the location of that line is not where it used to be.

On Health Care and the Social Safety Net

Perhaps the greatest disconnect between the Republican Party and scriptural mandate is their complete and utter willingness to provide aid to those in need.

There has never walked anyone on this earth who was a greater advocate for the poor than Jesus Christ and scripture is filled with references to the poor and our obligation to help them.

> [10] and if you spend yourselves in behalf of the hungry and satisfy the needs of the oppressed, then your light will rise in the darkness, and your night will become like the noonday. [11] The LORD will guide you always; he will satisfy your needs in a sun-scorched land and will strengthen your frame. You will be like a well-watered garden, like a spring whose waters never fail. (Isaiah 58:10-11 NIV)

> [27] Those who give to the poor will lack nothing,
> but those who close their eyes to them receive many curses.
> Proverbs 28:27 NIV)

I will not listen to those who fear God's anger over abortion or same sex marriage yet see no consequence for maintaining the belief that we just cannot provide health care to everyone, or insist that unemployment insurance, social security and Medicare should be dismantled.

What many people choose to ignore or simply not trust is the fact that when we lift up the lowest amongst us then it is to the benefit of all of us. There is in fact a real economic benefit to providing care for the poor.

Part of the Keynesian philosophy of economics is the belief that programs such as unemployment greatly decreases the volatility of our economy. It takes away the severe downturns that can devastate stability and confidence for years or even decades. By providing people with a safety net when an industry suffers, through unemployment insurance, food stamps, and Medicaid we reduce the effect that the loss of jobs in one particular industry has on other segments of the economy. When people are still able to buy food, clothes, or pay their mortgage the effect on the overall economy is mitigated.

Most liberals who understand this concept also realize there is indeed a certain moral obligation to help the poor as well.

Please pay special attention to the following message which is found in Matthew:

> [31] "When the Son of Man comes in his glory, and all the angels with him, he will sit on his glorious throne.
>
> [32] All the nations will be gathered before him, and he will

separate the people one from another as a shepherd separates the sheep from the goats. [33] He will put the sheep on his right and the goats on his left.

[34] "Then the King will say to those on his right, 'Come, you who are blessed by my Father; take your inheritance, the kingdom prepared for you since the creation of the world. [35] For I was hungry and you gave me something to eat, I was thirsty and you gave me something to drink, I was a stranger and you invited me in, [36] I needed clothes and you clothed me, I was sick and you looked after me, I was in prison and you came to visit me.'

[37] "Then the righteous will answer him, 'Lord, when did we see you hungry and feed you, or thirsty and give you something to drink? [38] When did we see you a stranger and invite you in, or needing clothes and clothe you? [39] When did we see you sick or in prison and go to visit you?'

[40] "The King will reply, 'Truly I tell you, whatever you did for one of the least of these brothers and sisters of mine, you did for me.'

[41] "Then he will say to those on his left, 'Depart from me, you who are cursed, into the eternal fire prepared for the devil and his angels. [42] For I was hungry and you gave me nothing to eat, I was thirsty and you gave me nothing to drink, [43] I was a stranger and you did not invite me in, I needed clothes and you did not clothe me, I was sick and in

prison and you did not look after me.'

[44] "They also will answer, 'Lord, when did we see you hungry or thirsty or a stranger or needing clothes or sick or in prison, and did not help you?'

[45] "He will reply, 'Truly I tell you, whatever you did not do for one of the least of these, you did not do for me.'

[46] "Then they will go away to eternal punishment, but the righteous to eternal life." (Matthew 25:31-46 NIV)

There are many on the religious right who will claim this message is meant for us as individuals and in no way should be taken to suggest that taking care of the poor is the responsibility of the government.

I would like to make two points in response to this. The first point is that there are many problems, especially medical problems that my neighbors may be faced with, that myself or for that matter, my community cannot afford. When a person is faced with a lifesaving transplant that will cost hundreds of thousands of dollars I cannot afford to take care of that person's bill, nor can many people or even whole communities. A bake sale just will not cover those costs. Medical care has advanced far past the use of leeches in treatment.

The second point I would like to make to these people is that if the numerous scriptures that deal with helping the disadvantaged in no way should be taken as a responsibility of the government, then why do you insist that the government must abide by what the Bible says about homosexuality and abortion?

You simply cannot have it both ways. Evangelical Christians should demand that our government create a system of universal health care in which people contribute when they can afford to do so. Not only should they demand it, but they should do so loudly. They should disavow any politician who does not support universal health care.

Pastors should stand up in their churches and look their parishioners in the face before they ask the question, "How can you call yourself a Christian if you cast a vote for a representative who will not stand up for the sick amongst us. If you do cast such a vote then you must bear the weight of all of those people who die every year because they do not have health insurance."

It is true that people really do die from not having health insurance. A 2009 Harvard Medical School study published in the American Journal of Public Health found that 45,000 people die every year from being uninsured.

What if this figure was an over-estimation of the numbers and they missed the mark by a wide margin and that in reality only 25000 people die every year from not having health care. Is this an acceptable figure?

What does this say about us as a nation that we allow so many people to die from no health care? Would Jesus say, "I understand, you just could not do it so I'm cool with it?"

The fact is we have a representative government. We send representatives to Congress to do our bidding. The fact that it does not take those representatives long to learn how necessary it is to do only the bidding of their high dollar campaign donors is beside the point. They are supposed to represent our values and our morals. If blocking access to health care is a priority of your representative I can in fact make some fairly strong assumptions, none of which would be good, about the values of the district that sent this particular representative to Washington to do their bidding.

Now, there are those who say that everyone already is covered in the United States. Anyone can go to the emergency room if they really need treatment.

First of all, they cannot go to the emergency room to get chemotherapy to treat their cancer nor can their children go to the emergency room to get tubes put in their ears. They can go to the hospital when the pain from the growing cancer inside their bodies is too much to bear. They have earned the right to receive a morphine injection for pain in an effort to ease their impending death.

Second of all, why would you protect a system that sends the uninsured to the emergency room for the flu when you can organize the system and send them to a doctor, which would be much cheaper for all of us? That makes absolutely no sense whatsoever. It is not even borderline stupid, it is stupid.

It is an incredibly inefficient system that Republicans profess their undying devotion to because they have no alternative to offer and they cannot support a plan put forth by a Democratic President. They hate health care reform because it is in their political best interests to hate health care reform.

Certainly the health care debate that began in 2008 proved to be a contentious one. Some have argued that the government must stay out of the health industry due to simply the fact that it is such a huge part of our economy.

Our economic future, I would argue, is the reason that the government must be involved, especially since a large portion of our budget is affected by health care costs. One of the largest reasons for our increasing health care costs is the profit motive for private health insurance companies. Remove the profit motive and you decrease the rise in health care costs. Once again we see an economic benefit for government coming to the aid of the needy.

Many say that a single payer system amounts to socialism. Call it whatever you want, the fact of the matter is that single payer health care is the only thing that will ever provide us with lower costs and a manageable system.

I do not and will not claim or advocate for this type of system in any other industry that is currently considered private industry. The big mistake is thinking that the private health insurance industry is somehow similar to the auto industry or the furniture industry or the electronics industry.

You cannot have a profit motive when it comes to health insurance. You cannot have a private insurance company in charge of your treatment options when they make more money by collecting your premiums, but denying you coverage. There is a built-in conflict of interests.

At the same time that the insurance industry makes more money by denying you treatment our health care providers make more money by treating you more often. The two are completely at odds with each other. We need to give our doctors an incentive to make sure they take care of you the first time.

The purpose of insurance is to reduce your individual financial risk by spreading it throughout a larger group of people. Therefore, the nature of insurance suggests that the larger the group of people the cheaper it is for everyone.

When advocating for a single payer system I do so because I cannot conceive of a larger group of people than everyone in the United States. By utilizing a single payer system we decrease the risk to each individual and therefore the cost, we take out the profit motive and the excessive overhead costs which include bonuses for millionaire and billionaire executives. The savings would be tremendous.

We pay nearly twice as much per person for health insurance as anyone else in the world. If we paid what the people pay in the next most costly health care system, we would each have roughly four thousand more dollars in our pocket every year. Can you imagine the effect on our economy if we each took that four thousand dollars and each year spent it on electronics, new couches, a nicer car, or home improvements. The benefits would be extraordinary.

The ironic thing is that even though we pay twice as much as anyone else in the industrialized world, we have one of the world's worst mortality rates and infant mortality rates. Our access to the health care system is appalling and immoral. Yes we have great doctors, but only some of us have access to them.

The first step I believe that we should take is to allow a Medicare buy-in for anyone. Medicare costs so much because it serves only our elderly. When you have a program that insures only those most likely to get sick it is going to cost a pretty penny. Therefore anyone of any age should be allowed to buy-in to the system, in other words, pay a premium and be covered by Medicare. That premium should cost what someone their age would be expected to pay. The difference for that person would be that he or she would not be paying for profits or high overhead. This would be a much lower rate. I feel I should have the right to buy into Medicare.

Republicans insist that I keep paying private insurance costs because those are the people who contribute to their campaigns and make them extremely wealthy after they leave Congress.

If we were allowed to buy-in to this program this would help secure Medicare because now you would have typically healthy people paying their fair share.

If tea party minded people claim the right not to pay for health insurance and stick the rest of us with their emergency room bills, then at the very least I should not have to keep paying unnecessarily exorbitant costs for my health insurance. I should have the right to pay lower costs for a program which is run by the Government.

This would not increase the size of the government. It does not create an additional department. It is utilizing an existing resource to lower the costs for the individual and reduce the costs for the taxpayer.

There is one additional benefit to a Medicare buy-in that is not discussed much. If we were allowed to do this it would absolutely explode entrepreneurship and small business growth in America.

Those who have great ideas or great motivation are certainly risk takers, but one risk many are not willing to take is venturing away from employer provided health care. Individual plans are too expensive, especially for someone trying to start a business. Not having health insurance is not an option for people who feel that it would be placing the health of their family in jeopardy. If allowing an affordable Medicare buy-in would allow just one person out of ten thousand to take the leap this would amount to thousands of new business start-ups which would employ potentially hundreds of thousands of full time employees in the future.

Republicans claim to be pro-business when in reality they are pro-corporation and pro-Wall Street. Democratic policies have always done the most to benefit the small businessman. We need to relieve business of the burden of being responsible for providing health care. I would also add that we need to combine Medicare and Medicaid to relieve states of the tremendous burden of managing health care for the poor and unemployed.

At some point working class Republicans must ask themselves if the party they support, which advocates policies which brutally and adversely affect their lives, have found the only way for you to vote for them is to use your Christianity against you and describe the policies of the Democratic Party as evil and unrighteous. If you will allow me to be a bit crude, are they scaring the crap out of you to earn your vote? In no way, shape, or form do the policies of today's Republican Party make sense for working class America.

About That Individual Mandate

There are certain potential perils that come with living in a free
society. I fully advocate for a free society, but I also acknowledge
that while this means we are free to pursue our individual dreams
we are also free to be lazy and irresponsible.

Those who attack the individual mandate are necessarily
advocating for the right of personal irresponsibility. While they
say the government should not make anyone do anything, they are
also saying that the rest of us must pay for their irresponsible
decisions. In essence they are placing a responsibility tax on those
of us who are able and choose to be responsible. They do this
when we pay higher medical costs associated with their non-
payment of medical fees associated with costly emergency
treatment. Because of another's irresponsibility, we are presented
with the bill. They do not even give us a thank you. Instead, they
call us unpatriotic and un-American because some wealthy donors
tell them that we are and it plays very well politically.

Some say that it is impossible for the government to regulate
non-action and question how somebody can be penalized for

doing nothing.

Let me suggest a possible scenario. A parent of a six month old decides not to feed their child for a length of time that is sufficient to cause the child to die from malnutrition or lack of food. Is the parent guilty of anything? Has he caused harm to another by his inaction? Yes, of course he has.

Here is another scenario. You enter into a contract for a service in which you the homeowner has promised to pay upon completion of a job which replaces the roof on his home. The contractor does a fantastic job and completes his work two days early. At this time the contractor presents you with a bill and you decide not to pay. Are you guilty of breach of contract even though all you are guilty of is not paying the bill? Of course you are. There will be and should be a penalty for your inaction. Through our legal system we are held accountable when we do not fulfill our obligations.

Rousseau wrote about *The Social Contract* in which he describes the relationship between a government and its people. This relationship can be unwritten, but the government has an obligation to fulfill the needs of the people. If that contract is broken then the people have every right to enforce the contract.

We also enter into a social contract with our neighbors. A contract that says we will do nothing that will harm our fellow neighbors.

When people take a risk and decide that they do not need health insurance for whatever reason, it is the rest of us who assume the majority of this risk. They could decide that they are young and strong as an ox and come to the conclusion that they are invincible. That invincibility is called into question when they are involved in a car accident which lands them in the hospital for three months, amounting to a bill in the six figure range, that they have no ability to pay.

Those services may end up being free to that irresponsible individual, but the hospital will not bear those costs. Those costs are transferred to those of us in the community who do have insurance or the means to pay through higher costs on our bills when we utilize the same services.

Irresponsibility is a reality in today's society. It should not be rewarded and responsibility should not be penalized which is what is currently going on in our health care system.

The idea that people do not inflict harm on others by not having health insurance is a myth. A myth perpetuated by people stubbornly clinging to a health care system for the sole reason that this is the way it has always been done.

When people are allowed to decide not to have health insurance, we have lost the ability to enforce a contract which says that people should not harm others financially or for any reason.

At what point does arguing for the status quo just become foolhardy and ignorant?

On the Rich and Money in Politics

Enough about the poor, what about the rich? Anyone who has
been through Christianity 101 will know the answer to this
question.

Let us defer to the guide book:

> "Do not store up for yourselves treasures on earth, where
> moth and rust destroy, and where thieves break in and
> steal. But store up for yourselves treasures in heaven,
> where moth and rust do not destroy, and where thieves do
> not break in and steal. For where your treasure is, there
> your heart will be also. (Matthew 6:19-21 NIV)

> [24] "No one can serve two masters. Either you will hate the
> one and love the other, or you will be devoted to the one
> and despise the other. You cannot serve both God and
> money.
> [25] "Therefore I tell you, do not worry about your life, what
> you will eat or drink; or about your body, what you will

wear. Is not life more than food, and the body more than clothes? (Matthew 6:24-25 NIV)

4 Do not wear yourself out to get rich;
   do not trust your own cleverness.
5 Cast but a glance at riches, and they are gone,
   for they will surely sprout wings
   and fly off to the sky like an eagle. (Proverbs 23:4-5 NIV)

What good will it be for a man if he gains the whole world, yet forfeits his soul? Or what can a man give in exchange for his soul? (Matthew 16:26 NIV)

9 Those who want to get rich fall into temptation and a trap and into many foolish and harmful desires that plunge people into ruin and destruction. 10 For the love of money is a root of all kinds of evil. Some people, eager for money, have wandered from the faith and pierced themselves with many griefs.
11 But you, man of God, flee from all this, and pursue righteousness, godliness, faith, love, endurance and gentleness. (1 Timothy 6:9-11 NIV)

17 If anyone has material possessions and sees a brother or sister in need but has no pity on them, how can the love of

God be in that person? [18] Dear children, let us not love with words or speech but with actions and in truth. (1 John 3:17-18 NIV)

[17] Command those who are rich in this present world not to be arrogant nor to put their hope in wealth, which is so uncertain, but to put their hope in God, who richly provides us with everything for our enjoyment. [18] Command them to do good, to be rich in good deeds, and to be generous and willing to share. [19] In this way they will lay up treasure for themselves as a firm foundation for the coming age, so that they may take hold of the life that is truly life. (1 Timothy 6:17-19 NIV)

The core economic Republican philosophy is called Trickle-down economics or Reaganomics. The argument this philosophy makes is that if you take care of the wealthy amongst us then they will use the abundance that they possess to lift up the rest of us. Their greed for more money will cause them to invest in more innovation and increase productivity thus providing the lowest amongst us with jobs.

Many of my liberal friends would describe this as pure unadulterated hogwash and they would be entirely correct in doing so. There is no evidence that this is a legitimate plan to create jobs. Although the unemployment rate under President Ronald Reagan did decrease, what we found when we sorted out the details was that by the end of his time as our President, incomes for the middle class when adjusted for inflation remained stagnant while the incomes and wealth of the richest Americans increased dramatically. As the saying goes, the rich got richer and the poor got poorer.

The fallacy in this argument is the fact that the "job creators" in our society have no incentive to create jobs or increase production if the mass of people are too darn broke to buy what they are selling. You can let them keep all their money and even give them double their money back and they will do nothing to create jobs if we are broke and cannot buy their goods or their services. Why would they? It makes no sense. Instead they will invest their money in other countries where the middle class is strong and growing like China. Why would you invest in the United States when everything the Republicans are trying to do means lower wages for the rest of us and an ever shrinking middle class?

Following the recent great recession, corporate wealth increased dramatically in 2010. Corporations were sitting on mountains of cash, but were not creating jobs. At least they were not creating jobs in the United States. Their increases in sales were overseas in countries whose economies were improving and not shrinking. Countries such as China were getting our products and our jobs. In this case, reality supports Keynesian economic theory and disproves trickle-down theory. There was no incentive to invest in the United States when our economy was so untenable so they did not invest.

A corporation's sole purpose is to make as much money as possible. Their purpose is not to improve the United States. Their purpose is not to create jobs if they do not have to. After our corporations cut back and downsized due to the recession, they learned how to improve efficiency and they were not going to increase their payroll if they did not have to. They were going to push their current employees to do as much as possible. They knew they could do this because many of their employees were happy just to have a job and a paycheck. They were more than willing to do the work of two people.

Gordon Gecko thinks that "greed is good." Jesus Christ, not so much.

As Jesus often liked to do, he shared a story with us:

> [15] Then he said to them, "Watch out! Be on your guard against all kinds of greed; life does not consist in an abundance of possessions."
>
> [16] And he told them this parable: "The ground of a certain rich man yielded an abundant harvest. [17] He thought to himself, 'What shall I do? I have no place to store my crops.'
>
> [18] "Then he said, 'This is what I'll do. I will tear down my barns and build bigger ones, and there I will store my surplus grain. [19] And I'll say to myself, "You have plenty of grain laid up for many years. Take life easy; eat, drink and

be merry."'

[20] "But God said to him, 'You fool! This very night your life will be demanded from you. Then who will get what you have prepared for yourself?'

[21] "This is how it will be with whoever stores up things for themselves but is not rich toward God." (Luke 12:15-21 NIV)

Although a pure free market system has little controls for greed, a mixed free market system like the United States should. Through regulations we seek to protect the citizenry from the corporations. We have regulations which seek to mitigate the effects of unrestrained greed while still allowing for the advantages associated with allowing people to use their innovations and desire for wealth as a motivating factor.

While conservatives kneel at the altar of corporations those very same founding fathers that they often invoke when they seek to justify their allegiance to the principals of small government had a bit to say about the threat that corporations represent.

Tea Party darling Thomas Jefferson who I lovingly refer to as T.J. had this to say, "I hope we shall crush in its birth the aristocracy of our moneyed corporations, which dare already to challenge our government to a trial of strength and bid defiance to the laws of our country."

Nor did James Madison give a rousing endorsement for

corporations, "The end of democracy and the defeat of the American revolution will occur when government falls into the hands of the lending institutions and moneyed incorporations."

Jesus showed great disgust with moneyed interests being perpetrated in places of worship.

> [13] When it was almost time for the Jewish Passover, Jesus went up to Jerusalem. [14] In the temple courts he found people selling cattle, sheep and doves, and others sitting at tables exchanging money. [15] So he made a whip out of cords, and drove all from the temple courts, both sheep and cattle; he scattered the coins of the money changers and overturned their tables. [16] To those who sold doves he said, "Get these out of here! Stop turning my Father's house into a market!" (John 2:13-16 NIV)

Although not exactly a disavowal of moneyed interests in government we can easily see a correlation.

For obvious reasons many people consider the floors of Congress to be hallowed ground, a place where our elected representatives gather to do the bidding of their constituents not their large campaign donors. Yet, in 1995 our current Speaker of the House John Boehner passed out checks to fellow Republicans from the tobacco industry on the floor of the House. This was being done shortly before voting on a bill to end subsidies important to that industry. I would say that this represents a conflict of interest.

Shortly after Representative Darrell Issa was elected as the new chairman of the House Oversight and Government Reform committee he sent out letters to corporations asking them what regulations they wanted Republicans to make disappear. Who is running this show? Yes, that was a rhetorical question.

I do not know if there can be two clearer examples of what our elected representatives should not be doing. I readily admit some of this happens on both sides, but state that wherever it may occur that it is morally repugnant.

When there is a higher purpose involved, money has no place. Where elected representatives are obligated to make decisions in the best interests of the people, money should have no influence. Votes should not be bought with donations to the campaign war chests of our elected officials.

I could go on and on, but no one says it better than the great Republican President Abraham Lincoln;

> "The money powers prey upon the nation in times of peace and conspire against it in times of adversity. It is more despotic than a monarchy, more insolent than autocracy, and more selfish than bureaucracy. It denounces as public enemies, all who question its methods or throw light upon its crimes. I have two great enemies, the Southern Army in front of me and the Bankers in the rear. Of the two, the one at my rear is my greatest foe. Corporations have been enthroned and an era of corruption in high places will

follow, and the money powers of the country will endeavor to prolong its reign by working upon the prejudices of the people until the wealth is aggregated in the hands of a few, and the Republic is destroyed."

Let us look at just a portion of what Lincoln had to say. "It (money powers) denounces as public enemies, all who question its methods or throw light upon its crimes." Is this not what is exactly happening today? Anyone who questions corporations and their government proxies, also known as Republican Congressmen, gets labeled as socialists, Nazi's, un-American and enemies of our country.

Conspiracy theorists are readily drawn to a black President with the middle name of Hussein. That is an easy target, but they are missing a real conspiracy and that is the influence of corporations over the people who are running our government. The threat that corporations will one day control our country is imminent and their power once obtained will be absolute and it will not be wrested from them without great effort and much upheaval.

There is no crime in being wealthy. There is no crime in wishing to provide a secure home and finances for your wife and children. We are not taught that money is the root of all evil, but rather that the love of money is the root of all evil. We must be able to recognize the difference and see the true motivations of our leaders.

I am not condemning all corporations. I realize the need for them and the benefit they provide. I am simply recommending that we be wary of ceding too much power to them. If they control the government then they control us as well.

On Immigration

Immigration also represents a hot button issue for Republicans. Their anti-illegal immigration stance is currently very popular with their base. It currently costs them little in votes in the short term but alienates segments of the voter population that they will need in the future in order to win a national election.

I was quite surprised when I discovered that there is plenty of evidence in the Bible to suggest that this war on immigration is not righteous or scriptural.

> [33] "'When a foreigner resides among you in your land, do not mistreat them. [34] The foreigner residing among you must be treated as your native-born. Love them as yourself, for you were foreigners in Egypt. I am the LORD your God. (Leviticus 19:33-34 NIV)
>
> [21] "Do not mistreat or oppress a foreigner, for you were foreigners in Egypt. (Exodus 22:21 NIV)
>
> [8] And the word of the LORD came again to Zechariah:
>
> [9] "This is what the LORD Almighty said: 'Administer true justice; show mercy and compassion to one another. [10] Do

not oppress the widow or the fatherless, the foreigner or the poor. Do not plot evil against each other.' (Zechariah 7:8-10 NIV)

Of course there is always an alternative viewpoint and an opposing scripture for those who do not agree with the concept of giving amnesty or even limited amnesty to illegal immigrants. They usually point to the following scripture.

> [13] Submit yourselves for the Lord's sake to every human authority: whether to the emperor, as the supreme authority, [14] or to governors, who are sent by him to punish those who do wrong and to commend those who do right. [15] For it is God's will that by doing good you should silence the ignorant talk of foolish people. [16] Live as free people, but do not use your freedom as a cover-up for evil; live as God's slaves. [17] Show proper respect to everyone, love the family of believers, fear God, honor the emperor. (Peter 2: 13-17 NIV)

So in this case we must obey the laws of the land which would take precedence they would argue. In other words even though we were commanded to be kind to strangers and foreigners by scripture, since illegal immigrants are here ... illegally as determined by our government, then we need to pack them on buses and get them the heck out.

To which proponents of amnesty will point out what we learn

from the Book of Acts,

> [27] The apostles were brought in and made to appear before the Sanhedrin to be questioned by the high priest. [28] "We gave you strict orders not to teach in this name," he said. "Yet you have filled Jerusalem with your teaching and are determined to make us guilty of this man's blood."
> [29] Peter and the other apostles replied: "We must obey God rather than human beings! (Acts 5:27-29 NIV)

Looking at this scriptural evidence we learn that God's laws are more important than man's laws so we should show kindness to strangers and forget about the laws of our government.

This is exactly what drives people mad about Christianity. Depending upon your own personal viewpoint you can twist or find support for whatever your position.

Often, people who support the toughest illegal immigration policy and suggest that we need to obey man's laws concerning immigration policy, will also completely disregard Jesus' message of compassion.

They would also argue that our laws must depict scriptural commands that they find in scripture such as abortion and marriage. Should they also not fight to make sure that our immigration laws more closely resemble scripture? They will not though, because they just do not care. These people represent the worst of Christianity. They will fight for and support only what they personally think is right even if they must do so without the benefit of a scriptural mandate.

They will stand up and say that a Pastor is obligated to stand up and tell their flock to vote Republican or vote for a candidate because it is God's will, even though it is certainly against the laws of our country for a pastor to advocate for a particular politician from the pulpit.

People who do not understand Christianity are bound to be confused. Where does it stop? Who do you believe and who do you not believe? When should we follow God's laws and when should we follow man's laws?

How can anyone definitively say that they are right and how the heck can anyone attack someone else as "un-Christian" for having a different view point? We are all trying to figure this out. Nobody knows anything for sure. We have the ability to speak of God, but we do not have the ability to speak for God.

How can you stand up and glorify the story of the Good Samaritan and insist on casting out illegal immigrants? You cannot.

Reread the following message in Exodus;

> [21] "Do not mistreat or oppress a foreigner, for you were foreigners in Egypt. (Exodus 22:21 NIV)

Why were they being told not to oppress aliens? Because they were once aliens themselves. The message is that we should remember where we came from and how we would have wanted to be treated.

Unless we have American Indian blood flowing through our veins we are all immigrants or children of immigrants.

The small minded response to this is, "Yeah, but they came here legally." Who cares? I am a citizen because I was born here. What a cakewalk that is.

Most illegal immigrants spent all they have and risked their lives because they wanted something better for them and their children. I am proud of the fact that people are willing to risk losing their life to be a part of our country and to live where I live. They have paid a far greater price to be here than I have, perhaps not a greater price than my ancestors, but a far greater price than myself.

Many people have discussed at one time or another a philosophical question which asks parents to contemplate what they would do if after falling on hard times they were left with the option of stealing a loaf of bread to feed their family or not steal and let their family starve. Most people state that they would steal the loaf of bread because they could not allow their family to go hungry.

Is this not what most of the men and women who cross our borders are essentially trying to accomplish? When leaving a country and a life that is often filled with pain, suffering, hunger, and violence are they not hoping for something better for themselves and more importantly their family? Should we not at the very least pause to consider their plight and be ever so grateful for our personal circumstances and bounty?

I have worked alongside of Mexican immigrants and I was left with a great deal of respect for their plight. They could outwork many from my community. As a result of my work ethic, I was able to forge a bond of respect with them, even if I could not understand much of what they said.

While I see so many young people fully engaged by little more than their XBOX or MTV I saw immigrants working, for the lack of a better word, their ass off trying to provide for their families because they do appreciate what we have even while many of us can in no way appreciate what we were born into.

The time has come to act with responsibility. This problem needs to be addressed immediately by people who know how to solve problems and not win elections. For those on the far right who envision bus after bus leaving the US and headed for Mexico to drop off our unwanted, think again. It will never happen. This concept has been a boon for Tea Party activists and really gets their juices flowing, but the majority of mainstream Republicans know a drastic solution will alienate a great many people and voters.

We do need immigration laws that start with securing our border, but we need a path to citizenship for those who are here doing the right things such as working and educating their children. We need to create a system where they can begin to contribute to society through paying Federal taxes.

The criminals amongst them must go. Yes, put them on a bus

and take them across the border.

Historically, the United States has imported a great deal of ingenuity and passion from other countries. Yes, under the current laws many have come here illegally, but the majority of them possess certain traits that are remarkably American; persistence, resilience, drive and the desire for something better.

The mighty Republican icon Ronald Reagan made this simple statement in a 1984 debate with Walter Mondale, "I believe in the idea of amnesty for those who have put down roots and lived here, even though some time back they may have entered illegally."

In 2010 we could not pass the Dream Act which creates a pathway to legalization for those who came to the United States before they were sixteen and after they completed two years of college or two years of military service. These are the kids and youth we should treasure. What a tremendous miscarriage of justice occurred when Congress failed to pass the Dream Act.

Politics must end on this issue and compassion must begin.

On the Environment

Concerning the environment, it should seem obvious that we are expected to take care of our planet. It was created by God and we are the caretakers.

> ³ Through him all things were made; without him nothing was made that has been made. (John 1:3 NIV)

God demands this from Adam;

> ¹⁵ The LORD God took the man and put him in the Garden of Eden to work it and take care of it. (Genesis 2:15 NIV)

> Also from Genesis;

> 26 Then God said, "Let us make mankind in our image, in our likeness, so that they may rule over the fish in the sea and the birds in the sky, over the livestock and all the wild animals, and over all the creatures that move along the ground." (Genesis 1:26 NIV)

We are the stewards of this earth. Despite millions upon millions of dollars spent by the pollution industry to dissuade people from believing in global warming, the evidence is empirical, conclusive, and legitimate scientists agree with the evidence. The planet is warming. I know the topic is laughable on Fox News, but this is no laughing matter.

Every time it snows, Fox News Hosts jump on the old "so much for global warming" bandwagon. They joke incessantly about it and mock those who believe the evidence.

Rational people, as in those who do not have a pollution agenda, understand that global warming is a matter of percentages of a degree over several years. Those minute changes though, are having a dramatic effect on our environment.

When I watched half-term Governor Ms. Palin chanting "drill, baby, drill" and "mine, baby, mine", I wondered if it would ever be possible for us as a nation and a planet to tackle the problem of the environment as if we were the stewards of this planet. It seems like we will forever be reliant on our addiction to fossil fuels. There are renewable energy sources and that is the way of the future.

One of the greatest problems I see with the whole global warming debate is the fact that because conservatives, oil execs and coal execs are able to find some scientists who believe that global warming is a sham that there are a great many people led by pollution advocates such as Sarah Palin, who think the quality of the air that we breathe does not matter at all.

The EPA should be abolished they say. Are you serious? The good that the EPA has done to protect our waters, our forests, our air and our communities should never be discounted.

The war on the EPA is entirely due to the fact that forcing industries to be responsible for the environment, costs them money. The corporations have a very real financial incentive to demonize the tree hugging liberals and a very real incentive to fill the campaign chests of people who care more about winning elections than making sure our children have clean air to breathe and clean water to drink.

Many will speak of our deficit and say how awful it is that we are going to hand this debt to our children and grandchildren. I will not argue that this is not awful, but I feel with equal conviction however, that it would be just as awful to hand our grandchildren a polluted planet, a planet where corporate profits takes priority over clean air and clean water. We can pay off our deficit if we act responsibly, Democrat Bill Clinton demonstrated this, but what we are doing to our planet is rapidly becoming irreversible. This problem will not be solved by throwing away our hairspray bottles.

I will agree that the planet can undergo changes in the environment on its own without our help. This fact, however in no way dispels the evidence that suggests we are actively doing harm to our environment.

The environmental movement started long before global warming was a part of our everyday language. It was important even before we suspected that collectively the billions of people on this earth with their actions might just be doing something that will have dire effects.

The belief that abolishing the EPA will work because industries will and can police themselves is tragically misinformed. If a company can save a million dollars by dumping chemicals in a river without fear of repercussions then they will dump chemicals in a river. Those rivers typically feed into the river systems of other states. Those smoke spewing power plants release pollution that is carried through the air to other states. This is exactly why we need federal intervention concerning matters related to the environment.

How amazing would it be if we had two parties who competed for the best ideas to preserve our environment instead of the Democrats repeatedly trying to push through environmental legislation and Republicans fighting them every step of the way?

I am going to ask those who think we should just get rid of the EPA and completely discount global warming the same question Christians often ask atheists. What if you are wrong?

Religion and Science

There has been a theory floating around with fundamentalists that I completely discounted the first time I heard it, but by the third time I heard this theory, I knew that many people took it seriously.

It is used to justify or rationalize prayer in school or the teaching of creationism. Their theory begins by providing the assertion that since evolution has the "missing link" that it cannot be proven. They also fully allow that they cannot prove creation theory. Since creationism and evolution are both theories then religion is the same as science and science is the same as religion. Since science can be taught in schools then religion can be taught in schools.

For those of you who have not heard this argument before now please feel free to take a moment and collect your thoughts before we move on. The sheer and utter ignorance of this argument can be mind numbing.

Let us begin at square one and draw upon the wisdom of Webster-Merriam.

Science is defined as:

1: the state of knowing : knowledge as distinguished from
ignorance or misunderstanding

2a : a department of systematized knowledge as an object
of study <the science of theology> b : something (as a sport
or technique) that may be studied or learned like
systematized knowledge <have it down to a science>

3a : knowledge or a system of knowledge covering general
truths or the operation of general laws especially as
obtained and tested through scientific method b : such
knowledge or such a system of knowledge concerned with
the physical world and its phenomena:

Religion is defined as:

1*a* : the state of a religious <a nun in her 20th year of
religion> b (1) : the service and worship of God or the
supernatural (2) : commitment or devotion to religious faith
or observance

Some may have thought that when you looked up
religion in the dictionary it said "see science" or when you
looked up science it said simply "see religion." If you read
the respective definitions you can see that this is not the
case.

The steps of the scientific method are as follows: ask a question,
do background research, construct a hypothesis, test the
hypothesis by doing an experiment, analyze the data and draw a
conclusion and finally communicate your results.

The steps for religious method if you will are: 1. Your pastor tells you what to believe 2. You believe it.

Science involves coming to a conclusion based upon real and observable results. Religion involves coming to a conclusion based upon ones faith and personal beliefs.

Scientists seek to either prove or disprove a theory. Pastors take religious doctrine and craft their version of reality around what the church has always preached as true. It is the proverbial problem of "teaching an old dog new tricks."

Most people and organizations do not want to admit that they are wrong and religious institutions have repeatedly demonstrated that this is true about them as well.

Scientists must admit that they are wrong when their hypothesis is proven incorrect or they cease to be able to be referred to as scientists. Being wrong sometimes offers value because at the very least you have learned one more thing it is not. There is value in information.

Pastors or believers on the other hand must never state that doctrines or church teachings are wrong or they are subject to possible excommunication in some of the most extreme churches.

Evolution is based upon generations of evidence and creation theory is based on a holy scripture.

Fundamentalists are attempting to use an absurd false equivalence to further their agenda and push their views on others.

The fact that all religion is based upon faith and not fact is not to be seen as discounting the value of religion.

For those of us who are religious the fact that we often talk about things that we cannot see or that science could never address is not a strange concept.

Science can and does explain things however, when there are observable results. When science can explain something that goes counter to what religious institutions believe we should not just discount the evidence and call it trash science.

Religion plays a central role in my life, yet I can separate science from religion and neither one has to be greater than the other.

They are two completely different animals, but there need not be a "survival of the fittest" battle between the two. They can and should, both be able to co-exist.

It is true that sometimes religion and science try to explain the same things, but they come to their conclusions through a different process. That process is what differentiates the two.

Abortion and the Idea that is the Wolf in Sheep's Clothing

I would like to make some people aware of a little fact that is not often discussed.

There are pro-life Democrats. Let me say it again, there are pro-life Democrats. Might I add also, that there are pro-choice Republicans. There is this misconception that all Democrats think alike on everything and that all Republicans think alike on everything. That is not the case; a politician often chooses to align themselves with the party that best fits their ideals and philosophies. It is not often a match made in Heaven.

It may just be a good idea for the pro-life movement if, instead of attacking all Democrats as evil baby killers, that conservatives embrace them and try to work with them. For any significant change to be made in regards to abortion it would take significant bi-partisan efforts.

Abortion is always an explosive and toxic social issue for politicians. Depending on which side you fall, you will lose or gain voters. Some people vote for President on just this issue.

They claim that the only thing God cares about is abortion which is ironic since Fundamentalists also claim that all sins are equal.

People on both sides of the issue will be quite irritated with my thoughts on how to best tackle the issue. Neither side will want to claim me.

Many consider the most important scripture related to abortion to be:

[13] "You shall not murder. (Exodus 20:13 NIV)

I do believe that when a woman has an abortion that they are ending life. I also personally believe that there is something inherently wrong with using abortion as a birth control method.

Under most circumstances I would not allow my underage daughter to have an abortion. In most circumstances I would counsel my grown children against an abortion if they were to seek my counsel. There is something inside of me that says that making this decision could affect you for the rest of your life.

Technology has gotten us to the point where we have on record a child being born and surviving after a shortened gestation period of twenty five weeks. Viability is most often determined as twenty four weeks. Many states severely restrict abortions after twenty four weeks and they do so with the blessings of the courts as long as they allow for abortions when the mother's life is in danger.

Approximately one percent of abortions performed today are considered late term. The greatest diligence must be used to determine the medical necessity of performing the abortion.

I personally believe that if there is a chance a baby can live outside of the womb then terminating the baby's life inside of the womb is tragic. I do not know how you can see it any other way.

There are many issues to consider concerning abortion, such as women who are victims of rape or incest and women whose lives are threatened by carrying the baby to term. The most ardent anti-abortionists do not believe in abortion under any circumstances, but the majority of Americans believe that at the bare minimum abortions should be allowed in cases of rape and incest, as well as when carrying the baby to term jeopardizes the life of the mother.

Where this issue is so contentious is that some women regard their own ability to maintain their own reproductive rights and control over their bodies as important as some women and men feel that abortion is wrong. We live in America. Freedom and liberty are obviously important issues for us whether we are male or female. Women see the government's intrusion into their lives, their bodies and privacy as denial of a basic liberty and as an affront to basic women's rights. I have come to understand that these women do and should, care deeply about their personal freedoms. The Republicans who lead the charge against oppressive abortion laws are usually women and rarely men.

I think those feelings must be respected. Some women do not want some old cigar smoking politician in Washington D.C. to enter into their relationship with their doctor. In the case where a mother's life is in jeopardy, then Washington and state politicians should have zero right to determine whose life is more valuable.

In regards to my personal opinion, I know I could never ever stop thinking about the potential that my baby had and was denied, by myself or the mother of my child.

When anti-abortionists speak of abortion as murder, and for the sake of this argument I am not questioning whether it is or not, I wonder if they really mean it.

Let us do a little experiment. Let us say that you have a sister who had an abortion. What would be your feeling about the matter? I allow that there are a very few who would never speak to this sister again. Most though, I feel, would look past this and eventually be accepting of their sister despite what she had done. Now, let us say that this sister had a six year old child. Let us say that this sister drowned this child in the bath tub. Would it now be a completely different story? You might get past this eventually and still love your sister, but your ability, if you are honest; to get over what she had done would become far more difficult.

Let us remove the family connection from the discussion. An acquaintance would like you to have lunch with her and be joined by a woman who you discover has had an abortion thirty days ago. Most would agree to this. What if you discovered that this woman is under investigation for the murder of her small child? I suspect that the lunch date would be off.

Let us do another experiment. If abortion were made illegal would you jail the woman who had requested the abortion?

Would you advocate for the death penalty since it would be defined as murder. There are those who would say definitely not. In fact one anti-abortionist that gets a lot of press says, "[If] you're asking, should anyone end up in jail for having an abortion, absolutely not. That's nothing I would ever support." That was Sarah Palin in her now infamous interview with Katie Couric that took place in September of 2008.

Now why would she say absolutely not? If abortion is murder then the mother of the aborted fetus should be tried as a murderer, and a woman who has several abortions performed should be considered a serial killer. As a serial killer, in some states the death penalty should be considered as a possible sentence.

The person most directly responsible for the abortion is the mother. It would not be performed without her willingness to do the procedure.

The fact is that most people draw a line between abortion and murder, whether this is appropriate or not.

Do I think that a woman who has an abortion is evil? No. Many have a difficult time forgiving themselves for what they have done. I think they should be supported and counseled if they are having difficulty. I do not think they should be jailed. This is not an unforgivable sin. What do you know, Sarah and I actually agree on something. Christ does guarantee us forgiveness of our sins, it is just people who do not forgive that have a hard time accepting this fact.

Most people do not realize that Sarah Palin has been under attack before by anti-abortionist groups who claim that she is pro-choice. In 2009 American Right to Life made this statement concerning Ms. Palin, in a report, "Her words and actions prove that she is officially pro-choice and stands against the God-given right to life of the unborn." This must have come as quite a shock to the woman who once claimed that you could not get any more pro-life than she was.

There are obviously lines drawn in different places by different people. Everyone has a different sensitivity level to the abortion issue and the fact that there is a group out there that describes Ms. Palin as pro-choice is evidence of this.

The idea that I feel is the wolf in sheep's clothing is the Republican obsession with Roe-V-Wade. I sincerely believe that the fact that the key component in the minds of pro-life advocates is Roe-V-Wade has contributed to more abortions being performed than if they tackled the issue in a different way.

If you were to ask people what happens if the Supreme Court were to overrule Roe-V-Wade a shocking sizable percentage would look at you like you were stupid and inform you that abortion would be outlawed.

This would be correct to a point but it is not as simple as that. Some states have existing laws on the books that would allow abortion to be criminalized virtually immediately. Many states would have to enact new legislation if they wanted to criminalize abortion.

I have read estimates that anywhere from 10 to 30 states would criminalize abortion. I think that the thirty state figure might be a little high. Thirty is a number put out there by both pro and anti-abortion groups. Pro-choice groups probably like a higher estimate because it motivates likeminded people to be active and pro-life groups would like a higher estimate because it perpetuates the idea that most people are in favor of criminalizing abortion.

Even though I do consider myself pro-life, in no way shape or form do I want to see abortion outlawed. In case your jaw just dropped and you spit out your coffee, I'll make sure you heard me right. I am unequivocally and unapologetically against making abortion illegal and therefore for securing a women's right to choose. How can that be you ask? I will explain it to you if you promise to keep an open mind.

Before Presidential elections you see a great many protestors holding up signs that say "end abortion" or "stop abortion". If you think that outlawing abortion will end abortion or stop it, then you think the war against drugs has worked and ended drug use in the United States.

It is not because I do not think that women should have a choice to have an abortion, because I do, it is that I think they will still have that choice and make that choice whether it is legal or illegal.

There will be no stopping or ending abortion. Let us say that Roe-v-Wade is overturned and your state decides to make abortion illegal. On the night before abortion was made illegal in your state there will be much celebrating and praising of God by all of the Christians who fought the "good" fight. What you should be doing is getting some sleep because you just made your job ten times harder.

The abortion clinics will have gone from the medical facilities with signs out front to hotels, dorm rooms and boyfriend's bedrooms. You will no longer know where to picket with your signs. The people performing the abortions are not going to ask your daughter if she has the necessary permission from her parents. They are not going to suggest your daughter wait twenty four hours so that she has time to think about it. They will tell your daughter however, to give them two hundred dollars before they get started.

The black market is remarkably efficient. When licensed facilities are shut down then criminals will move in to fill the void. The abortions will be performed by college medical students to help them get through school, or they will be performed by anyone with a computer and who is enterprising enough to access the internet and instruction manuals.

Here is a homework assignment. Google "do-it-yourself abortion" or "how to give yourself an abortion" and see what you come up with. Sometimes the mother will take it upon themselves to do this.

Every teenager will know someone who knows someone who

knows how to perform an abortion. In exactly the same type of referral system for high schooler's that use drugs, young girls will now have the ability to have an abortion that is cheap, can be hidden from their parents, and is quick. In many ways young girls will find this a far superior option than discussing it with their parents and actually going to a clinic.

Seventy percent of the population in Brazil is Catholic. One thing no one can deny is that the Catholic Church forbids abortion. They are very vocal and powerful voices against abortion. Abortion is illegal in Brazil except for cases of rape or when necessary to save a mother's life.

I can actually give you some personal insight into how strict Catholics have been in the past. Before I was born my mother had a pregnancy in which the child died while still in her womb. As a good Catholic back in the sixties she was forced to carry the baby until the body rejected the pregnancy. For at least five months she had to carry the fetus knowing it was dead. When the baby was finally rejected, the loss of blood almost killed my mother. If that had been the case I would not be here today. Just take a moment to ponder this. Can you even imagine what it would have been like to be in my mother's shoes? My mother's teeth began to decay and her back broke out in acne. This is not a healthy situation for a woman. This is definitely a case of where the Church's stance almost prevented the birth of another.

In March of 2012, the Georgia House passed what had been

labeled the "Women as Livestock" Bill. The original wording of the Bill said that it would be unlawful to have an abortion after twenty weeks for any reason, even if the fetus was dead.

Republican Representative Terry England reasoned and implied that if farmers had to "deliver calves, dead or alive," then human women should have to do the same thing. I do not make this stuff up. This is the Republican Party today. Even though the original wording was changed after the resulting uproar and did not make it in the final bill you can see where the Republican Party wants to take us.

They want to take us in the direction of Brazil, who is actually contemplating taking another direction. Despite the predominately Catholic population in Brazil, they are currently undergoing a serious debate to legalize abortion or at the minimum to expand the existing laws to allow more abortions.

Why? Because it is not working. The abortion rate in Brazil is extremely high. Due to the illegal status of abortions women have turned to other means. Figures from 2004 estimated that less than 200 legal abortions had been performed in Brazil, yet the total number of illegal abortions was closer to one million. Hospitals are being overrun with mothers suffering from uncontrollable bleeding. The problem is serious and making abortion illegal is seriously not working.

There are multiple methods that women use to perform abortions. Some take poison, some insert items into their uterus and some use trauma against their stomach. The most often used method in Brazil is one that is picking up popularity in the United States in poorer communities. The FDA approved ulcer drug Misoprostol is also used to induce labor. Used in early labor however, it will induce miscarriage by bringing about uterine contractions and the ripening of the cervix. In the US it is used in conjunction with RU-486 to improve the effectiveness of the "day after" solution.

It can cause massive bleeding leading to the death of the mother and in cases where the use of the drug does not completely work, it can cause birth defects in the child. Yet women consider it a real alternative to carrying the baby to term in a country that has made abortion illegal.

Cost of one dose in the United States is two dollars. Studies in New York have shown that its use is growing due to its low cost and they do not need to fear the stigma associated with visiting an abortion clinic.

Pro-life advocates will just say that they will make the "day after" drugs illegal. It is currently manufactured both in the United States and overseas. Make it illegal and it will still be purchased on the black market. If police are as good at eliminating the supply of banned Misoprostol as they are at Cocaine and Heroin, women will have no problem getting this drug and can probably get the required dose within an hour.

Now let us look at a country where abortion is both free and legal.

The Netherlands abortion rate is routinely the lowest or near the lowest in the world. This is true in spite of the fact that abortion is both, free and legal.

They do still have restrictions on abortion. In practice they do not perform abortions after twenty one weeks although the official limit is three weeks higher at twenty four weeks.

How is it that their rate of abortions is so low if it is free and legal? They have created a culture of family planning and vigorously supported the use of contraceptives.

I know it is a bit cliché by now, but it is true that the number one cause of abortion is unintended pregnancy.

I find it difficult to listen to people who are opposed to abortion, yet maintain that abstinence is the only morally relevant and acceptable message to deliver to children. Birth control is a "no-no" they say. I am not going to get into this much, but when I looked for scriptural, especially New Testament, support for the anti-birth control crowd I found it extremely lacking, in fact, almost nonexistent.

Until we start impressing upon our children the importance of being responsible and explaining that not being responsible will have an extremely dramatic effect on the rest of their lives we will not get anywhere, whether abortion is illegal or not.

When we start teaching our teenage daughters that the time for starting a family is still several years off in the distance we will be getting somewhere. Daughters should be instilled with self-respect inspired by parents who are comfortable to let their children venture into the world to pursue their own dreams and make their own decisions.

We run into a problem brought about by living in a free society once again. We have an environment in which people are able to turn on MTV and see teen pregnancy glorified or watch extremely sexual behavior on reality shows. To permit this and then deny teenagers access to birth control and tell them abstinence is the only way is irresponsible. Yes, you may not let your kids watch shows such as I have described, but your neighbors on both sides probably do. On some level legislating morals derived from religion, through the government is incompatible with living in a free country.

Now let us see how the abortion rates of The Netherlands, Brazil and the United States look when stacked up next to each other. The Netherlands typically comes in around 13 / 1000 pregnancies. The United States comes in around 22 / 1000 pregnancies. Estimates for Brazil typically come in around twice the United States rate, as high as 40 / 1000 pregnancies.

Which result would you prefer?

Another factor that undoubtedly increases the likelihood of abortions is lack of access to decent health care coverage. How many abortions are performed for the sole reason that people would rather have an abortion now than be faced with the medical bills that could reach tens of thousands of dollars if the baby is carried to full term?

A responsible approach to the abortion problem would be to reduce or eliminate as many of the reasons people have for having an abortion, yet Republicans will fight to the "death" to make sure that millions of Americans are denied health coverage.

When more of us realize that it is not just one way or the other, and there is possibly a third way or a fourth way we just might be getting somewhere.

If you are of the same opinion as I am that it is not only pointless, but foolish to make abortion illegal then Christian fundamentalists will now declare you evil. Saying that you do not want to make abortion illegal to Christian Fundamentalists, means that you are okay with abortion. For many of us, nothing could be further from the truth.

If you are of the same opinion that I am, that abortion as birth control is inherently wrong on a moral level, but you will not deny women the right to choose then the ultra-left will attack you.

Saying that you think abortion is wrong and reasonable efforts should be made to discourage the practice to the left means that you are taking away the personal freedoms of women.

It is all or nothing for both extremes and then there is everybody else that is stuck in the middle. Many of whom, quite frankly think both sides are nuts.

Opinions are a dime a dozen concerning abortion. Many feel

strongly about their opinion. Obviously, people feel that their opinion is right or at least that their opinion is right for them.

I am not arguing that you should agree with my point of view. I am simply suggesting it just might be possible to allow another person the ability to have their own opinion without painting them as evil or horrible people.

To quote Barack Obama, "no one is pro-abortion."

There are no bells and whistles that go off at an abortion clinic when an expectant mother walks in. Nobody hands out party favors. Nobody is out there romanticizing abortion. To a person, everyone thinks that this is a serious issue.

I do believe that a person's faith has an impact on the decisions we make. Perhaps it might be better to concentrate on spreading the message of Christ's love to as many people as possible instead of expending the majority of our effort trying to change the laws of our government which has proven to be woefully ineffective at curbing other sins.

There are sensible solutions and room for compromise even though both sides will say that there is not.

I would argue that, perhaps if we did compromise a bit, we can create an environment where our abortion rate is the lowest in the world and should that not be the ultimate goal.

Hate Masked as Righteousness is Still Hate

In May of 2012 Barack Obama became the first sitting President to come out in favor of same-sex marriage. It was a brave move and an important first step. With that step the Democratic Party entered the 21st century, whilst the Republicans seek to go back to the 19th century. I applaud the President for his actions and the courage it took to make this decision and the announcement.

During the lengthy debate over the military's "don't ask, don't tell" policy it was quite surprising to discover that an overwhelming majority of Americans supported the repeal of DADT. This represented significant progress in the way we think of gay/lesbian members of society.

Despite this progress, personal opinion concerning same-sex marriage is lagging behind. Fundamentalist Christians say you just cannot allow man to marry a man or a woman to marry a woman.

My first thought of this attitude is, what do they care what someone else does and who are they to say what someone else can or cannot do. This is nothing like the health care individual mandate. It is very easy to demonstrate the damage done by others when they irresponsibly do not carry health insurance, but same sex marriage hurts no one. We cannot just make up laws limiting the freedom of others just because we do not like them or what they do in their own home. This is a free country, isn't it? The only basis for denying them the right to marry comes from a moral opinion that results from a person's religious beliefs. In a country where the separation of church and state is the law of the land how can we possibly deny somebody anything and use religious beliefs as justification. This is a civil rights issue.

There is an easy answer to the mystery of why they care so very much and it is their belief that if we as a nation allow gay marriage then God will punish us and throw down fireballs upon us or maybe he will just inflict us with natural disaster after natural disaster. Once again, after the emergence of Jesus Christ and the New Testament we are taught that things were not going to work that way. It is simply more attractive and exciting for some people to believe in a vengeful and spiteful God instead of a loving one.

If you ask me if the Bible does say that homosexuality is an abomination then I would have to say yes.

Yet, just as I have seen news stories that make a fairly compelling argument that some people are born in the wrong sex I do believe that some people are born gay. I believe that most of us have been able to sense that someone is gay while the individual is still very young. People whose brothers and sisters are all heterosexual will sometimes be gay. One half of a twin might be gay while the other half is straight. Because brothers and sisters are raised in the same environment, this would suggest a lack of a correlation between how a person is raised and who they are attracted to.

We know by now that many fundamentalists have low regard for science or any manner of intellectual thought, but the overwhelming evidence is that people are born gay. It is not a choice for people that are homosexual anymore than it is a choice for me to be a heterosexual.

An argument that used to work well with me was that homosexuality goes against nature. A fundamentalist Christian belief that many learn from a young age is that homosexuality is unnatural. My own instinct suggested that this was obvious.

I believed this until I read an article titled "Homosexual Activity among Animals Stirs Debate" for National Geographic News by James Owen from 2004. This article says that there are several species of animals which engage in homosexual behavior including sheep, fruit bats, dolphins, and orangutans.

Many will ask, "How dare you compare human beings to a fruit bat?" I would first tell them to calm down and then explain that I am not comparing human beings to fruit bats. I bring this into the conversation for the simple reason that I had once thought since there were no examples among other animals of homosexual behavior then I could justify saying homosexuality is unnatural. I can no longer say this. If one asks the question does it go against nature, now I understand that it does not. You may argue that it does go against human nature, but how many centuries and millennia with an ever present existence of people with a homosexual orientation does it take to at least say it does not go against the nature of some?

I do not believe being gay is a choice. Because I believe this then I find it difficult to paint these individuals as an abomination and have difficulty believing that there should not be a place for people who are LGBT in today's Christian church. Because of this I will not hate them.

Many fundamentalist pastors will tell you that they love gay people and that they have held AIDS patients in their arms while they were dying. Usually they will manufacture some tears for effect. They will do this while they preach against gay marriage and against including members of the LGBT community in hate crime legislation.

For many if not most fundamentalist this is their banner issue. This is the issue they hang their hat on. This is what their ministry is all about. Such pride they must feel to be able to spend their lives pushing certain members of society and their friends and family who love them, away from the church.

They could very easily go the rest of their lives without saying one word about gay people and instead stress the hope, the comfort, and the security that faith in Jesus Christ offers.

What follows is an argument that fundamentalists should consider. By excluding members of the LGBT community from their churches they give up an opportunity for the power of faith in Jesus Christ to transform a person. Many people will never walk into a church because they feel that they are not welcome. Many will shut down and stop listening once a person says they are a Christian because they have been treated so horribly by "Christians" in the past.

We are indeed all God's children. Deny it and you deny truth.

I try to imagine if Christ would jump right in and agree with virulently anti-gay politicians such as Rick Santorum and Michele Bachman. Would he be involved in the hate speak? I cannot fathom that he would do anything, but rebuke their behavior and their language.

This is a personal observation, but it seems apparent that many fundamentalists isolate themselves from others which gives them a false impression that all Christians think like they do. Many tend to only surround themselves with likeminded people. A practice that is about as un-Christian as anything I could think of.

Thankfully there are thousands of pastors that welcome gay members with open arms. There are a few Christian denominations that allow gay pastors. The United Church of Christ, Methodists, Presbyterians and Episcopalians all can have very liberal views toward homosexuality.

Fundamentalists will say that these denominations and their teachings are wrong, evil, dangerous and incredibly ill advised.

I would argue that they simply think differently and that is just fine. They still welcome people into their church. They still introduce people to Christ. Is that not the most important thing?

Not everyone is alike. If the only thing out there for people were fundamentalist Christianity then there are many people who would never consider Christianity. Churches that reach a group of people that fundamentalist Christianity does not, should be embraced and encouraged not maligned and hated.

For many Democrats the debate over whether being gay is a sin is inconsequential. They have separated church from the state and the state from the church.

It is possible for some people to preach against homosexuality in their home to their children and in their churches or even take that message to their neighbors and friends, but still recognize that their personal opinion based upon their religious beliefs should have no bearing upon how the government rules if we are to maintain a free society.

This represents a fundamental belief that discrimination against anyone, for any reason, is wrong. It is a matter of the Constitution, freedom and liberty. This is an entirely American concept.

It is why we can be adamantly opposed to discrimination based on race, but allow that the KKK should have the right to exist and that the government should protect that right.

Many people, including myself, find it rather ironic that many people will argue for protecting the institution of marriage from gays and lesbians, yet heterosexuals have shown nothing but total disdain and lack of respect for the institution of marriage as evidenced by our fifty percent divorce rate. Heterosexuals, including myself, have made a mockery of the institution of marriage and have reduced it to nothing less than a contract too easily broken.

Some people argue on behalf of civil unions, allowing that gays and lesbians should be afforded the same rights but not be allowed to call it marriage. I do not know that this is an acceptable compromise. How can you legislate a word or prevent people from still calling it marriage? Furthermore, who cares?

I personally believe that no church should be forced to recognize gay marriage or perform gay marriage ceremonies and I believe that many fear that this is what will occur. This provision is not necessary, nor would it be Constitutional.

If believing that there should be no discrimination based on a person's sexual preference is the worst thing we are guilty of then so be it.

I personally do not find it imperative to my "Christian-ness" to tell a homosexual that they are an abomination. I do find it imperative that I tell anyone open to listening, of the love and hope that awaits them if they will listen and follow the words of Christ.

I would think that if you are one of the people who believe that homosexuals are an abomination then every effort should be made to lead that person to Christ and if you believe that Christ is all-powerful then his message and his spirit should be more than enough to affect the kind of change you desire.

> ¹⁹ Though I am free and belong to no one, I have made myself a slave to everyone, to win as many as possible. ²⁰ To the Jews I became like a Jew, to win the Jews. To those under the law I became like one under the law (though I myself am not under the law), so as to win those under the law. ²¹ To those not having the law I became like one not having the law (though I am not free from God's law but am under Christ's law), so as to win those not having the law. ²² To the weak I became weak, to win the weak. I have become all things to all people so that by all possible means I might save some. ²³ I do all this for the sake of the gospel, that I may share in its blessings. (Corinthians 9:19-23 NIV)

This passage says to me, and other translations will further suggest, that you do not win converts by placing yourself above a person or by attacking a person. You win converts to Christ by showing empathy and by showing understanding. Those who insist on telling homosexuals that they are an abomination and expect them to respond, "Oh really, I better stop." are fooling themselves and have more than likely built a road block in the path of a person who may have found Christ if not for their tactics. Those who deny Christ to anybody will one day receive their very own special judgment.

> 2 You, therefore, have no excuse, you who pass judgment on someone else, for at whatever point you judge another,

you are condemning yourself, because you who pass

judgment do the same things. (Romans 2:1 NIV)

Recently a number of suicides by gay high school students has drawn national attention to the problems associated with bullying. It has long been known that kids can be cruel. The results of that cruelty can even result in causing a young man or woman to hate themselves and their lives so much that they choose to end the pain by taking their own life.

Of course Christian dogma teaches us that suicide guarantees that individual a place in hell, so many people then struggle with the concept of their son and daughter or brother and sister sitting in hell for his or her actions.

It is difficult to reconcile this position when we think of a loving and compassionate Jesus Christ. People who have committed suicide have quite often suffered through terrible lives and endured much misery. Happy people do not kill themselves.

There are many biblical scholars and experts in the field that say the translation concerning the evils of homosexuality is suspect. Considering that the concept of a homosexual orientation was not even discussed until the mid-1800's it would not be that big of a leap to think that the New Testament writers had no frame of reference that would allow them to be accepting of homosexuality or even capable of understanding homosexuality.

At different points in history the church has taught us that the sun revolved around the earth and that the earth was flat. They were wrong. One day there will be an entire world that will remark how odd it was that people once discriminated against people who were homosexual.

By choosing to focus on the compassionate words of Christ we lose the impulse to establish with complete certainty which sins and which acts guarantee us a place in hell.

Those high school bullies have learned their behavior. We are not born knowing who to hate. We are not born with a lust for prejudice, discrimination and condemnation. Someone must tell us who to hate. Necessarily the biggest impact on children and their beliefs and subsequent behavior are their parents.

Should we blame the kids or do we blame us?

The Fallacy in Santorum's "Family" Argument

Before the final results for the 2012 Iowa caucus were fully tabulated, Rick Santorum delivered what I felt was an effective speech, a speech that played very well with middle class Americans.

A Rick Santorum candidacy would be a "family values" candidacy. The family unit is extremely important to working class America. It is to these working class voters he was addressing and referring to when he said;

> "They share our values about faith and family. They understand that when the family breaks down, the economy struggles. They understand when families aren't there to instill values into their children and into their neighbors as Little League coaches, as good neighbors, of fathers and mothers being part of a community, that the neighborhood is not safe and they are not free. These are the basic values that American's stand for and these are the values that we need if we are going to go up against Barack Obama and win this election and restore the founding

principles of our country to America."

The implication is that the Democrats are responsible for broken families. If the breaking up of American families is truly the cause of our economic failures, which is an incredibly weak argument, he may want to point his finger at Republicans like himself.

What he fails to mention is that the reason that the parents are not there to instill values into their children and coach their baseball teams is because those mothers and fathers are working their ass off. While Republican governors such as the likely former candidate for President Rick Perry seek praise for their ability to create minimum wage jobs, the people working those jobs realize they simply do not pay the bills. They need two of these jobs and their wives need one and none of them provide adequate health care.

It is hard to make sure your kids do their homework when you can barely keep your eyes open. It is hard to know what your kids are doing at night when you are in the middle of your second shift of the day.

Since the 1970's when the work force was thirty percent unionized and the middle class was strong we have followed the Reagan model of trickle-down economics and declared war on unions. The result is that we have a shrinking middle class and stagnant wages, wages barely able to keep up with the cost of inflation. Today we have roughly eleven percent of Americans in unions and some Republicans fighting to eliminate the minimum wage.

In this same speech Santorum spoke fondly of companies like Wal-mart because they do not ship their famously low wage jobs overseas, ignoring the fact that a large percentage of the products sold by Walmart are made overseas.

Republicans think that the only way we can compete with foreign manufacturing is to drive down wages. Let the race to the bottom of the pay scale begin. This is how we win, this is how corporations improve profits and this is also how the middle class disappears.

The economic stress experienced by American families has wreaked havoc on their ability to stay strong and stay together.

Santorum must be confused unless he feels that personal bankruptcy and the subsequent moral bankruptcy that often occurs, are the values that people want to bring back to America.

Knee Jerk Politics and Income Inequality

Republicans are very effective at being able to place their talking points on bumper stickers. Their message often does not have any substance or supporting evidence to back up their assertions, but they are able to strike a chord on a basic emotional level with a certain segment of our population.

Democrats on the other hand often need people to think a little bit more in order for them to understand both, the implications of Republican policies and why Democratic policies would benefit them more. Many voters either do not have the patience to take the next step or they do not trust anyone who asks them to take that next step.

The dilemma for Democrats, often is, how do they counteract Republican rhetoric that is designed to bring about that knee jerk response from voters.

Let us look quickly at the example of income equality. Much ado was made out of the January 2012 Pew Research poll concerning income inequality, "two-thirds of the public (66%) believes there are "very strong" or "strong" conflicts between the rich and the poor--an increase of 19 percentage points since 2009."

While other polls came out stating that income inequality was not an issue with the majority of Americans, I feel that most would agree that the majority do not see worsening the divide between the rich and the rest of us as a good thing.

Republican's love talking about a flat tax or at the minimum, a flatter tax, but they never seem to talk about the real implications for working Americans. The knee jerk response from their base is excitement, which results in complete devotion to the cause. What could be fairer than everyone paying the same percentage of their income for federal income taxes?

Meanwhile the ultra-wealthy campaign donors who we can envision sitting along the bar at the club smoking cigars and drinking scotch, are equally amused and amazed that their Republican friends have managed to convince a sizable portion of the masses to believe that crap.

According to an article from Forbes, Newt Gingrich's tax plan would have exploded our national debt by nearly one trillion dollars the first year it would have been enacted. In the article written by Howard Gleckman he states, "...and while most of the nation's lowest-income families would get no benefit from these tax cuts, the top 0.1 percent (who make an average of more than $8 million) would get about a quarter of the windfall, according to new estimates by my colleagues at the Tax Policy Center."

Reuters reported that Mitt Romney's plans had only a slightly smaller impact on the deficit, but would still raise it by 600 billion dollars. According to the article, "wealthy taxpayers in the top 0.1 percent of earners would get an average tax cut of $482,940 in 2015."

To demonstrate a contrast, in the same article from Reuters Obama's tax proposals, which includes extending the Bush tax cuts for the middle class, but ending the cuts for the wealthy, would reduce the deficit by 312 billion over the next five years.

When you look at the Republican's plans what you see is the wealthy keeping more of their money as a percentage of income, while the lower income levels are less dramatically affected either positively or negatively. Once these programs are implemented then the gap between the wealthy and the poor necessarily has to increase.

Once these Republican programs are implemented and we end up with the results of an exploding deficit then they will say that we have to make dramatic cuts in our spending. The only thing that there is to cut are programs that help students, the poor and our senior citizens. When those programs are cut then the income inequality gap necessarily has to increase.

When you make Federal Income tax more flatter and you fail to realize that the other taxes we all pay including social security, property taxes, and sales taxes are regressive in nature, meaning people who make less are more adversely effected, then you have further stacked the deck for the wealthy. The income inequality problem is not made better by Republican policy, but is made increasingly much, much worse.

Anyone who votes has a decision to make. Do we take what a politician says at face value, or will we take the effort required to make an informed intelligent decision? The last thing Republican's want you to do is think about what they are feeding you.

Politics may be fun for some of us, but the results will have a profound effect on our lives and the lives of our families. This is certainly not a game, but a great deal many of us have been played.

What the Rest of Us Fear

There are two terms that all of us should become familiar with.
The terms are Reconstructionism and Dominionism.

Reconstructionism traces its roots back to Calvinism and was first
made popular by a gentleman named Rousas John Rushdoony.
Reconstructionists believe that everything including our
government, our Constitution and our elected officials should act
in complete submission to the Bible. They hold the laws of the Old
Testament to be just as valid as what is taught in the New
Testament. Of course when they are talking about the Bible they
mean their very own special interpretation of the Bible.

They call this ideology found within the Christian Evangelical
movement, theonomy. Among other things they believe in
criminalizing homosexuality and adultery, the gold standard,
extremely limited taxation and the elimination of all entitlements.

They are intolerant of all other religions and feel that the rights
defined under the Constitution only apply to Christians.

Some people use Reconstructionism and dominionism as
synonyms. They are in fact very similar although dominionism

can trace its roots a little farther back.

Dominionism received its name from a passage from the King James Version of Genesis:

> 28 And God blessed them, and God said unto them, Be fruitful, and multiply, and replenish the earth, and subdue it: and have dominion over the fish of the sea, and over the fowl of the air, and over every living thing that moveth upon the earth. (Genesis 1:28 KJV)

They believe that this passage suggests that Christians have dominion over everyone and everything including governments.

With this type of belief system it is easy to compare extremist Muslims and extremist Christians. They both think the same way and see anyone who does not believe what they do as the enemy.

It can accurately be said that Reconstructionism is a modern strain of dominionism.

Dominionists believe that God's laws should take priority in secular society. They believe strongly that we were founded as a Christian nation and that we must return to being a Christian nation.

What do we have to fear from these two very similar ideologies? Right now nothing, but what we must consider is that we had two prominent candidates for the Republican Presidential nomination that are heavily influenced by Reconstructionist leaders. Michelle Bachmann and Rick Perry make no excuses for their faith. Nor should they, but they must answer questions about whether they believe their faith or rather their interpretation of the Bible will take priority over the United States Constitution.

In an article written by Frank Schaeffer, whose father was once considered a leader of the Dominionist movement, he describes a very real threat to our democracy. From the article *Michele Bachmann Was Inspired By My Dad and His Christian Reconstructionist Friends -- Here's Why That's Terrifying;*

> "The message of Rushdoony's work is best summed up in one of his innumerable Chalcedon Foundation position papers, "The Increase of His Government and Peace." He writes, "The ultimate and absolute government of all things shall belong to Christ." In his book Thy Kingdom Come— using words that are similar to those the leaders of al Qaida would use decades later in reference to "true Islam" — Rushdoony argues that democracy and Christianity are incompatible: "Democracy is the great love of the failures and cowards of life," he writes. "One [biblical] faith, one law and one standard of justice did not mean democracy. The heresy of democracy has since then worked havoc in church and state. Christianity and democracy are inevitably enemies.""

There was a very real concern that should Bachmann or Perry have won the election and become President of the United States that our democracy as we define it would be in danger of being changed forever. This is more than just some conspiracy theory.

Essentially there was a fear that the goal of the two fundamentalist candidates was to change a government "by the people, for the people" to government by Christianity for Christians. If you have the same opinion concerning the inerrancy of the Bible then this may not strike you as a problem.

If the Bible is truth then why should this be a problem? The simple answer is that we only thrive as a nation due to "rules" outlined in the Constitution of the United States.

Many of our original settlers came to the East Coast of America to escape religious persecution and by the time of the signing of the Constitution there were many prominent factions of Christianity. Some of the cosigners of the Constitution questioned the existence of God.

Having a theocracy as a form of government causes innumerable problems. At some point our forefathers decided that religion's place was not in government and government's place was not in religion.

A state religion or a state mandated religion goes against everything we were taught to believe in. When one religion is preferred then other religions suffer. Government telling Americans what to believe would be oppressive. Government allowing Americans to believe whatever they want represents liberty and freedom.

Freedom of religion was not considered crazy in the beginning, it was accepted and it was understood that it was imperative to assuring the freedom of all.

I myself pray that our leaders make decisions based on an exceptional standard of morals. Often times these morals are learned in Church. I do not suggest that those decisions be mandated by Christianity or any other religion.

I pray that Christianity be taught in our homes, not in our schools. I do not want some teacher that I know nothing about empowered to answer questions from my children about what it means to be a Christian. I pray that the spread of Christianity is accomplished by messengers of the good word and not mandated by my Government.

When did freedom to worship as one pleased become not good enough? It is an amazing right that we have. It is a right that we should have. When did it become acceptable to some, for our government to tell people what to believe?

In the 2008 election much ado was made of President Obama's relationship with his pastor Jeremiah Wright who preached some questionable sermons and on occasion used inflammatory rhetoric. The associations of Rick Perry and Michelle Bachmann should be subjected to the same scrutiny.

Including in your spiritual advisors people that suggest that our Democracy would be better served by Christians and only Christians, than the wishes of the people defeats the purpose of why our Democracy exists. We are a grand experiment. Whether we exist five more years or five hundred more years will be determined by our attitudes.

Will we be determined and vigilant in maintaining the freedom of everyone or will we become lazy and naive.

Will our actions be a response to fear or will our actions be dictated by belief in an idea and the continued advancement of issues important to the progressive movement.

A Sense of Entitlement

Getting people to understand that the social safety net is a good thing for everyone -- even the wealthy, and our economy -- is not difficult if your audience is willing to take the time and listen with an open mind.

The problem many people have with entitlements is the idea of people continuously working the system and living off the state and thus the taxpayers for a large portion of their lives. They fear that once their children learn this behavior they will grow up and act in the same manner, which would create a vicious cycle. A learned entitlement mindset would create a problem.

My practical reply is this: Undoubtedly this is occurring on some level and will continue to occur. Some people will continue to live off the system and never give it a second thought. Nothing will change this and nothing ever will.

Fraud and abuse of the system must continue to be ferreted out and punished. New systems and technologies must continue to be developed that are able to track individual trends and provide prompts or red flags to the enforcement community.

The safety net is designed to get people on their feet after a difficult time. We cannot throw the baby out with the bath water. This is an important service and one that helps immunize one sector of the economy from the losses associated with another sector of the economy.

Do we eliminate the system so we can make sure that no one is abusing the system? No, we absolutely cannot afford to do that.

I admittedly have a far kinder view on those that are struggling in this society than my conservative friends. I perceive that the percentage of people who enjoy living off of the state is very small.

In conversations with friends I know that some stay on unemployment when a job is available because the unemployment checks are larger than what they would receive in their paycheck.

Therein lies the problem. The vast majority of us would strive to get off of government assistance, but more and more people are giving up hope. They are giving up hope because the path to real opportunity keeps getting smaller and smaller.

Every time Republicans cut spending on education a portion of the American dream dies. Every time Republicans strike down equal pay laws, a portion of the American dream dies. Every time a Republican succeeds in weakening the power of unions, a portion of the American dream dies. Every time Republicans eliminate or weaken child labor laws, a portion of the American dream dies.

If Paul Ryan and Republicans were to succeed in eliminating

Medicare, senior citizens will have no security in their final years, and a portion of the American Dream would die.

If Republicans were able to do away with the minimum wage requirement like many are seeking to do, we will have lost all sense of decency, and a portion of the American Dream would die.

Republicans are systematically dismantling the American dream and they are doing this under a false banner of patriotism, a non-existent endorsement by God and by labeling everyone else as socialists.

Sometimes all a person needs is a dream to keep fighting. Kill the dream and you kill the spirit.

The apparent Republican goal to lower our worker's wage rates and benefits to a point where we are competitive with China's wage rates should not be what we strive for.

This is America. We should use innovation to create new industries and new markets, markets where the prevailing wage rate can be higher than in other industries. We should invest in our youth and their education to create a pool of talented, industrious and passionate workers who deserve wages commensurate to their value to the work force.

If Democrats are not willing to resort to the tactics of the Republican Party and paint all Republicans as American dream "killers," then they better start presenting themselves as the great protectors of the American dream.

Election 2012: The Secret Muslim vs The Boring Mormon

By the time of the writing of this chapter we have all discovered that Mitt Romney truly was the inevitable nominee. His organization and his money resources far outclassed the competition.

With a President that some will claim is a secret Muslim right after they get done berating him for attending a Christian church for many years which was led by a controversial pastor and an opponent whose family history has been associated with the Mormon faith for generations, it will impossible to take religion out of the equation for the 2012 election.

Many fundamentalists consider the Mormon faith to be a cult. I get a chuckle every time I hear this and they explain what characteristics they use to base their conclusion when determining that Mormon equals cult. Every single one of those characteristics can also be used to describe the Christian faith.

Many evangelists and fundamentalists will eventually endorse Romney, choosing to vote for the devil they know rather than the devil they do not.

For a religious community that considers the Republican Party to be endorsed by God and Jesus Christ, I am wondering if that means that we should all become Mormon. The three candidates who had claimed to be called to run by God, Rick Santorum, Rick Perry and Michelle Bachmann all would lose to the Mormon Mitt Romney. What does that mean? Should Fundamentalist Christians not consider Mormonism to be endorsed by God? It is a bit of a predicament they have themselves in. Of course there is no community of believers who can rationalize their viewpoints and votes like Fundamentalist Christians.

So what is Mormonism? Many are completely ignorant of what the church believes and stands for. The sum of most people's knowledge is that in the traditional Mormon faith men could have multiple wives.

Mormonism dates back to the 1820's when a man by the name of Joseph Smith had a vision. In the vision Smith believed that an angel led him to a book written on golden plates. The book told a tale about an ancient people. After the book was translated it became known as the Book of Mormon. The Book of Mormon is just one of a few additional scriptures that they claim and follow as opposed to traditional Christians.

Mormons do claim to be Christians and place Jesus Christ at the center of their religion. They also believe that prophets and apostles can and do live today. Such prophets and apostles are able to speak the word of God.

In the Mormon Church the youth are given positions of responsibility at an early age.

They hold themselves to very high moral standards. Their moral standards are stricter than most Christians I know. They have a code associate with health and do not permit drinking of alcohol or caffeinated drinks. They also do not permit sex before or outside of marriage and passionately oppose adultery.

The official name of the church is the Church of Jesus Christ of Latter-day Saints and will excommunicate anyone who adopts the fundamental Mormon practice of a man having more than one wife.

They have a long history of being persecuted by their neighbors as well as our government. Despite this, they are not a cult and members are not the boogeyman.

They are upstanding citizens who are dedicated to their religion and maintaining the high moral code their religion mandates.

I probably should disclose my loosely based association with the Mormon Church.

When my son Tyler was seventeen years old he began researching the Mormon faith and their history. He would eventually visit their local church and was embraced by their community. He would soon become baptized and an active member. Shortly later his brother Dylan would do the same.

I completely and fully supported their decision. I attended Tyler's baptism, but was unable to attend Dylan's because of another commitment.

Of course the church asked if I had any interest in their faith to which my reply was no I do not. They respected my decision and were very grateful and a little surprised that I was so supportive of my children.

Many others thought I was crazy and I should put an end to it. I heard the "cult" word multiple times. It struck me when visiting the church during baptism and for a service, that everyone was very normal and very pleasant. To a one they were all very good people and extremely dedicated to their faith. Most were highly intelligent and successful in their careers. I had absolutely no problem with my son associating with these people.

What else factored into my decision? Well, he was seventeen. He was going to be out of the house in a few months and could do whatever he wanted to at that point and because he was seventeen the surest way to make the Mormon Church even more attractive was to tell him he had to stay away. How many centuries of parents raising rebellious teenagers has to take place before people realize this fact?

Today, neither son is officially a member of the Mormon Church, yet both maintain ties that may last their entire life. I am indifferent as to whether this is a good thing or a bad thing. I am certain that there are others who think this is a great turn of events.

Obviously I do have a liberal take on a variety of issues which includes the separation of church and state. I believe this separation should and will be maintained despite the efforts of many to remove the separation. Because of this I am less concerned with the chosen religion of a potential President than others may be.

A candidate's religion though, and their devotion to it can demonstrate a high capacity for morals and the ability to make decisions based on beliefs that are ingrained in the core of their being. That can be a good thing or a bad thing.

I have no problem with Romney's Mormon faith and his faith alone would never disqualify him as a being a potentially great President.

His policies, his positions and his ability to change his positions do however disqualify him as being someone whom I would want to see lead our nation.

Debbie Wasserman-Schultz, a Congresswoman from Florida and the chair of the Democratic National Committee has already stated that the Democrats will not play the Mormon card.

I pray she is right. Democrats and Progressive Christians must behave in a manner that is respectable. We must hold ourselves to a much higher standard than every Fundamental Christian I have ever met.

In short we must practice what we preach. We must be open-minded. We must love our neighbor whether they are Christian, atheist, Muslim, Buddhist or Mormon.

If we do this we pay tribute to Jesus Christ and his message. If we do not, then we are no better than they are.

By the Way We Also Celebrate the 4th of July

As I have already mentioned, I practice a liberal theology, but many who think like me also have liberal social ideals and adhere to a liberal economic philosophy. I am a liberal and a proud liberal. Call me a progressive if you will, but do not do so because you think I may take offence at being called a liberal.

For certain elements of society the word liberal has become interchangeable with such words as communist, socialist and fascist. We are dangerous individuals who should never be trusted.

While liberals such as myself choose to align themselves ideologically with such historic figures as Franklin Delano Roosevelt, Robert Kennedy, and Martin Luther King, many would suggest that each of us tree hugging "ne-er do wells" have a secret room with a secret wall painted red and devoted to displaying pictures of Hitler, Mussolini and Lenin.

On a day such as the 4th of July, when we should all celebrate our nation and some of us recount historically accurate stories of our nation's birth, there are members of society who find it difficult to imagine that it would be possible for self-styled liberals, progressives and Democrats to find cause for celebration on the Fourth of July.

This all too common charge that those like us are unpatriotic and un-American is an allegation that I take great umbrage with.

By definition conservatives and liberals do not think alike and that is just fine. The idea, however, that liberals are unpatriotic is absurd. Those who say such things are guilty of one of two things, they are either ignorant or they are lying with the intent of influencing your opinion so that it more closely resembles their opinion.

Liberals do find it difficult to stomach the assertion that our founding fathers believed that there is an inherit bias toward discrimination in the documents and actions produced by those very same founding fathers.

I will allow that the 3/5 compromise which allowed for slaves to be counted as 3/5 of a white man for the purpose of determining a states representation in Congress, and the lack of a provision guaranteeing women the right to vote were monumental fails in regards to discrimination. The need to compromise to achieve a bigger goal allowed for these fails to exist.

Time, acquired wisdom, and progress would eventually fix these wrongs.

Liberals respect, honor and cherish the Constitution as an evolving document capable of being changed when we as a nation are ready for change.

We believe that the founders had it right when they said in the Declaration of Independence, "We hold these truths to be self-evident, that all men are created equal, that they are endowed by their Creator with certain unalienable Rights, that among these are Life, Liberty and the pursuit of Happiness."

We acknowledge conservatives love the Constitution as well. Well, they love certain parts of the Constitution. Different conservative groups would love to repeal a variety of amendments including the 8th, the 14th, the 16th, the 17th, the 19th and possibly the 26th amendment.

Liberals do believe that children born in the inner city or poverty stricken rural areas deserve the same access to health care as blue bloods spending the holiday on Martha's Vineyard. We are not unpatriotic because we believe this. Perhaps you could call us compassionate, but not unpatriotic.

We understand that we pass on more to our children than just budgets and balance sheets. We also pass on the environment and the planet to those who come after us. Regardless of whether or not we feel that global warming is real or a myth we still value clean water and clean air.

We may not appreciate the wars we are currently fighting in the Middle East, but we love and respect our soldiers. After all they are our brothers, sisters, mothers, fathers, wives and husbands.

We believe that teachers, policeman and firefighters should be paid and paid well due to their value and service to our community.

We believe that all of our children deserve libraries, gym class, and the opportunity to star in their school play.

We believe our country is great because we are a melting pot, not in spite of it. We value diversity. This is the American Way. This was the American dream.

We pay our taxes, but think that the wealthiest amongst us and the most profitable industries can share in bearing a little extra burden to fix our government's mistakes.

We believe that our senior citizens are people who have served our countries and their families well. They deserve not just our respect, but the ability to retire with the reasonable assurance that their health needs and financial needs will be met.

No, we do not agree with everything and much of the time we do not agree with anything, but it is not necessary to call each other unpatriotic or un-American. Liberals do not think conservatives are evil necessarily; we just think they are wrong. Perhaps some of the name calling conservatives out there will learn that liberals are Americans too.

What will I be doing this 4th of July and every 4th of July that follows?

More than likely my children and eventually my grandchildren will wake me up early so that we can go to the local parade, but before we leave for the parade I will hang our flag outside.

I am assuming and hoping the day will be filled with at least two Italian sausages smothered in onions, one elephant ear, and multiple lemon shake-ups. At the parade I will shake hands with a few elected officials, but offer my support and encouragement for those politicians that are Democrats. In my part of Indiana, they need all the help they can get.

I will conclude the day by watching the local fireworks display right before rushing home to put the kids in the tub so I can clean off the cotton candy that has become caked on their faces. With any luck I will not have to get out the tweezers to remove a roasted peanut from the ear of a child too young to know better.

We will go straight from the tub to the bedroom where we will sing songs and the kids will say their prayers before being tucked in and given strict orders to "sleep tight and don't let the bed bugs bite".

So what do liberals do on the 4th of July?

Pretty much the same thing everyone else does.

Conversation with Christ

There are so many people out there who I just want to shake back to reality. I want to tell them that it is okay to take care of others. That the central message of Jesus Christ is not everyone for himself and you will never win an argument with someone who differs from you through hate.

Forcing someone to observe Christian rituals and making them pray will not create Christians. Instead it creates very, very angry people who will become emboldened and energized against the cause of Christianity.

Infighting amongst the various churches who will seek control of the theocracy they wish for would be incredibly tragic. It would definitely not be the first time blood will be shed in the name of Jesus Christ.

It is time to stop being foolish and wake up. Oh yes, I did indeed call such notions foolish. There is an entire segment of the population out there that thinks a Jew or a Hindu and of course Muslims should not be allowed to hold office by virtue of their religion. That is not my America. That is not the founding father's

America. America is a free society for all, not a free society for Christians.

I would want no part of this proposed country that people like Michele Bachmann and Rick Perry suggest and yearn for and for which they hoped to earn people's votes. No part.

If you are a fundamental Christian and you have managed to keep your lunch down and have made it this far into the book please hold your indignation in check, at least for as long as you continue to support politicians that want to give the wealthy more money and eliminate Medicare for senior citizens. Please hold your indignation in check while you support needless and senseless wars that kill hundreds of thousands of innocent human beings.

How do you fix this problem when there are so many scared little sheep out there who believe everything that comes out of the hateful mouths of people claiming to be righteous? Quite frankly in a free society you cannot completely fix the problem. There will always be people on the fringe of society that are close-minded and love to judge and condemn others. It makes them feel special and better about themselves. There will always be lazy and ignorant people who prefer to have a pastor tell them what they are supposed to do instead of reading the Bible to find out what Jesus Christ wanted us to do.

If Christians ever coalesce and become determined to spread love and not hate, encouragement and not judgment they will win the hearts and minds of so many more people. Those people are desperate for something more, but invariably get something much less.

If Pastors eventually come to the conclusion that there are enough messages relating to the hope, compassion and forgiveness of Jesus Christ in the Bible for a thousand Sundays without ever having to push a political agenda the pews will be filled.

When Christian parents stop telling their children that being gay is an abomination, then their kids will stop going to school and bullying other kids who are homosexual and those kids will stop hanging themselves.

We are not mandated to tell people that they are an abomination, but we are mandated to be kind. We must treat others like we would want to be treated or else we miss out on the essence of what being a Christian truly means. We can talk about the wrath of God or we can talk about the forgiveness that Christ offers.

I do want my politicians in church. Not at the pulpit but in the seats beside me. Hopefully they will learn the values and morals that are necessary to lead our communities and our country.

I would rather suspect my Pastor's political leanings than have all doubt removed.

If Jesus Christ were to walk into many of today's churches to find politicians stumping for votes from the pulpit he would be appalled. Like the money changers they would be banished and the Pastor's who allowed it would be rebuked.

If we were to become a theocracy and Christians ruled the country by virtue of their religion do you not think that they would become consumed by the power of their position and corrupt in their actions? Of course they would.

If you were to go to Jesus Christ and say "Look Jesus, our rulers are all Christian and we teach our kids Christianity in school." Do you not think he would ask, "Why do you need politicians to teach your children Christianity? I convert these souls your government does not. Thanks to you, everywhere there are people who hate Christianity because your "holy" government mandates it. Do you really think the power of the Holy Spirit is so weak that it needs man's laws to perpetuate faith in God? Seriously, has everyone lost their mind?"

If you then implored him and said "Look we made abortions illegal, aren't you proud of us?" Would he not say, "Abortions are occurring everywhere and in greater numbers, but you do not know it because you have closed your eyes to it and thought the job was done because your government now handles everything. It was more important for you to pat yourself on the back for being righteous than to create real effective solutions. You should have used your time to spread the word to as many people as possible."

"But we made gay marriage illegal?" Surely he will be happy with that. He responds, "Half of you "straight" people get divorced. You have made a sham out of marriage."

And then if he asked the question, "Do you treat others like you would like to be treated?"

After a moments thought our imaginary church member would likely reply … "Ummm. I do if they are Christian."

"Is that what I did?"

"I'm sorry I'm confused. I don't think my pastor has really clarified that."

"What does your Bible say?"

I imagine Jesus walking over and picking up a dust covered Bible and wiping it off. He blows across the top and dust goes flying.

"Oh, well I don't read it much, I guess. My pastor puts up scriptures on the screen at church. He picks the best ones."

"No, he picks the ones that support his opinions. It would have served you much better if you read the Bible yourself."

"He's a real smart guy. He studied the Bible at college and everything."

"Is he God?"

"No. Of course not."

"Then he is fallible."

"But he's really, really smart. I trust him."

"You should have trusted me."

Putting Christ Back Into Christianity

Although I am currently without a home church, I have certain thoughts about what my ideal church should look like. I would love for it to be informal, without an identifiable leader and I would love it if I was told to leave my wallet at home.

The same church that distributed the anti-Obama flyers, I discussed earlier in the book, decided it was necessary to make sure that everyone knew that the ten percent tithe obligation must be a tithe to the church. In other words it is not five percent to your favorite charity or the local homeless shelter and then five percent to the church. No, it was ten percent to the church and then if you wanted to give to charity above that amount, then it would be fine with both him and God.

I understand a church requires structure and a leader. This is the nature of any organization. Of course once you have a leader, a building and several big screen televisions you need to raise funds.

There is a movement among some to worship in small groups, in living rooms where people gather to offer praise, express thanks, experience fellowship and learn from the trials and tribulations of others.

Although this usually is a precursor to the establishment of a permanent church, this is pretty close to what I envision. I find it difficult to believe that Christ, who railed against the religious establishment and the hypocrisy of the Pharisees, wanted his followers to create a structure that was exactly the same in function.

What if Christ in reality expressed his desire for others to spread the word and not build the church?

Spread the word about a new way of life, a new way of thinking about others and about God. A new way that was not restricted by Old Testament rules, but rather by just one rule, love everyone. Love everyone and in all instances, treat others the way you would want to be treated.

This way is open to everyone and does not involve a secret rite, but just knowing in your heart that Jesus represents truth and that truth is love. That love is available to anyone who is open to it. That love does not discriminate against people based on the color of their skin, the way they talk, who their parents are, whether they are rich or not, or who they love.

One thing that is certain is that a sizeable percentage of the church's in existence today have forsaken Jesus' advice about loving everyone and reserving judgment for himself. This includes churches led by people with last names such as Robertson and

Hagee.

Churches such as these are not houses of worship, but rather monuments to the egos of their pastors and tributes to doctrines and dogmas that run contrary to the current popular "What Would Jesus Do?" sentiment. Doctrines and dogmas whose greatness is determined only by their ability to endure and not because of any faithfulness to the message of Christ.

Some time ago, I believe it was over the uproar of Wal-Mart instructing their employees to offer greetings of "Happy Holidays" instead of "Merry Christmas," right wing conservatives declared there was a war on Christmas.

Shortly thereafter, shortening Christmas to Xmas soon became blaspheme and the need to put "Christ" back into Christmas has now become a popular Facebook meme.

This mythical war supposedly started by an employer choosing to acknowledge that other religions exist has been used ever since by Republicans to inflame their base and motivate them not just to vote Republican, but also to play a part in influencing others to do the same thing.

Much ado was made of "Obama's" Christmas tree tax, which amounted to less than a single quarter, fifteen cents per tree to be exact. This tax was requested by Christmas tree growers so that they could run a campaign similar to the "Got Milk?" campaign. I think anyone could see that this makes sense, yet Republicans took advantage of the fears of their base when they declared it represented conclusive evidence of the supposed war on Christianity and Christmas.

How beautiful this works out for Republicans. Who does not love Christmas after all? Since Obama leads the war on Christmas, it furthers the idea that Obama hates Christians, Christianity and anything American. He probably does not even like apple pie and if he did like it Republicans would feel the need to remind you that his wife would not let him eat the pie.

Pastors love to talk about rules and what we should not be doing. They like condemning people to Hell, which is a heck of a way to maintain job security. They love to talk about a vindictive God who lashes out at his believers and uses hurricanes to inflict his punishment and many in the pews will sit there and eat it up. They love it. Their pastor has given them permission to hate and tell other people they are not as good as them.

If Jesus really did show up in one of today's churches, the people in the pews would neither recognize him nor like him. If he stood up and talked about feeding the poor or caring for the sick they would call him a socialist or a fascist.

I call on all progressive or liberal Christians to stand up and be heard. People will not know we are out there unless we stand up to today's Christian right zealots and bigots.

It is up to us to spread the truth. It is up to us to stand up for the ideals and mission of Jesus Christ.

Today's Christian "leaders" have dropped the ball and because of this the body of Christ suffers. These pastors must become victims of their own conceit.

It is time for all of us to put Christ back into Christianity.

Message to my Children

As a parent of grown children and children still growing, the material and message contained in this book is very important to me, but I must recognize that my children may not hold the same opinion.

I love my children, but I understand that my views are my views and may not be theirs. Perhaps this is a crucial difference between a liberal and a conservative. A liberal allows for a diversity of thought, a conservative allows for nothing else.

Is there a framework that I would like them to work within? Yes, and what follows is a letter from me to them detailing the knowledge I would like all of them to have when they leave my house.

Dear kids,

I love you. The bottom line is that I love you. No matter what, I love you. I have and will make mistakes as a father just as you have and will make mistakes as children, but I can promise you that I will never make the mistake of not loving you.

My love will never be withheld or used as a tool to insure that you conform to my ideals. I will always encourage you to think for yourself. My spiritual path has been long and winding, yours may be just as long. I was entitled to take that path by myself and I assure you that I intend to allow you to have that opportunity as well.

While you "find" yourself, I encourage you to always err on the side of compassion, tolerance and love. Never exclude anyone from your life because they look different than you do or talk different than you do or think differently than you do, or even because they pray differently than you do. Rather, embrace everyone because we are all God's children and we all deserve to be treated with respect and love. Everyone has something to teach us.

Jesus commands,

[7] Dear friends, let us love one another, for love comes from God. Everyone who loves has been born of God and knows God. [8] Whoever does not love does not know God, because God is love. [9] This is how God showed his love among us: He sent his one and only Son into the world that we might live through him. [10] This is love: not that we

loved God, but that he loved us and sent his Son as an atoning sacrifice for our sins. [11] Dear friends, since God so loved us, we also ought to love one another. [12] No one has ever seen God; but if we love one another, God lives in us and his love is made complete in us. (1 John 4:7-12 NIV)

This scripture makes it clear that it is all about love.

We do not learn just from books or from people that teach from books, I want you to go outside and experience nature. In nature we can be closest to God's amazing works. Do everything you can to make sure your children, my grandchildren, are left a planet where they can breathe fresh air and drink clean water.

Love your country. In the United States we know freedoms that people in other countries can only dream of. It is true, men have fought and died to protect those freedoms.

We are the melting pot of the world. Where we once took pride in being the country where people would come to pursue the American dream, now it seems there are those who are scared of people who do not look like them or talk like them.

You should never fear the traditions of others. Experience different cultures and expand your consciousness. When in Rome...

Stand for something and never allow the weak to be oppressed by the strong. Never accept that needless suffering is justified or righteous and never trust anyone who says that it is.

Not everyone will like you. Accept that now. It was Winston Churchill who said, "You have enemies? Good. That means you've stood up for something, sometime in your life."

Work hard and whatever you do, do it to the best of your ability. You will go far if you never let anyone else outwork you. Early in life you may start out working jobs that are menial, but unless you do those jobs well you might not be trusted to do jobs that are more challenging.

Although work is important, play is important as well. Learn to relax and you will live longer. Laughing when you do not want to laugh, is often the best medicine. Appreciate the time you have with your family and friends. It is true that we do not know when they might be gone from our lives.

Apple's Steve Jobs knew a great deal about dealing with personal struggles. His cancer diagnosis made him think about death, but more importantly it made him think about life. In 2005 he said the following in his commencement address.

No one wants to die. Even people who want to go to heaven don't want to die to get there. And yet death is the destination we all share. No one has ever escaped it. And that is as it should be, because Death is very likely the single best invention of Life. It is Life's change agent. It clears out the old to make way for the new. Right now the new is you, but someday not too long from now, you will gradually become the old and be cleared away. Sorry to be so dramatic, but it is quite true.

Your time is limited, so don't waste it living someone else's life. Don't be trapped by dogma — which is living with the results of other people's thinking. Don't let the noise of others' opinions drown out your own inner voice, and most important, have the courage to follow your heart and intuition. They somehow already know what you truly want to become. Everything else is secondary.

We definitely do not have much time on this earth. It would seem that if we are supposed to do anything rewarding with our life it must be to make the lives of those around us better. The point of life cannot be to live in misery or make others miserable. Instead be happy, make those around you happy and do great things.

If you remember nothing else from me I want it to be this. Love others and do so extravagantly.

www.ingramcontent.com/pod-product-compliance
Lightning Source LLC
Chambersburg PA
CBHW060843280326
41934CB00007B/894